A
N
N
A
M

O
S

NDO - CHINA

Saigon

VA

EASTERN HEMISPHERE

Showing position of the
Burma-Siam Railway

RUSSIA

TURKEY

CHINA

JAPAN

ARABIA

INDIA

Burma-Siam
Railway

PACIFIC
OCEAN

PHILIPPINES

MALAYA

AFRICA

GUINEA

INDIAN

AUSTRALIA

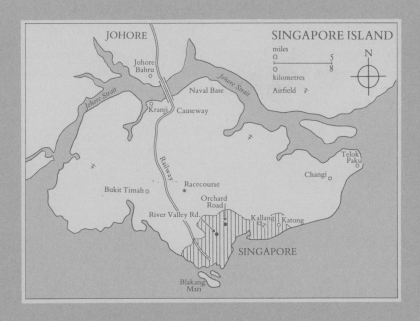

JOHORE

SINGAPORE ISLAND

miles
0 ————————— 5
0 ————————— 8
kilometres
Airfield

N

Johore
Bahru

Johore Strait

Naval Base

Johore Strait

Kranji

Causeway

Telok
Paku

Railway

Changi

Bukit Timah

Racecourse

Orchard
Road

River Valley Rd.

Kallang

Katong

SINGAPORE

Blakang
Mati

The Burma-Siam Railway

The Burma-Siam Railway

The secret diary of Dr Robert Hardie 1942-45

IMPERIAL WAR MUSEUM

Published by the Imperial War Museum, Lambeth Road, London SE1 6HZ

Copyright © Elspeth Hardie 1983
Foreword and Introduction © Trustees of the Imperial War Museum 1983

Designed by Herbert and Mafalda Spencer
and printed in Great Britain by
BAS Printers Ltd, Over Wallop, Stockbridge, Hampshire

Maps by John Flower

Thai Diddle Diddle poster p. 141 Dr Dudley Gotla
Wonder Bar and *Night Must Fall* posters pp. 141 and 143
Professor Hugh de Wardener
All other illustrations Elspeth Hardie

ISBN 0 0901627 26 7

Frontispiece: Robert Hardie as a captain in the Federated Malay States Volunteer Force, 1940

Contents

Foreword

The publication by a national museum of a highly successful series of books is a phenomenon worthy of some comment. This is the sixth volume of personal experience accounts of the two world wars published by the Imperial War Museum and, like the previous five, it was written by a man whose war was, in some senses, unexceptional. Yet Dr Hardie writes of his own unforgettable and awful experiences with a lucidity, elegance, and balance which brings home the nature of events at least as strongly as any more comprehensive historical account. The great value of all the books in this series is that they throw new and frequently unexpected light on broadly familiar history and this is perhaps the key to their success.

It goes without saying that we can only publish such accounts if we receive them in the first place, and I am most grateful to Mrs Elspeth Hardie for offering her late husband's remarkable record to the Museum. The Department of Documents is always pleased to accept unpublished diaries and accounts, whether they be of prisoners of war in the Far East or of other theatres of war. We can only publish a very small proportion of what we take in, but everything is carefully preserved and made available to scholars and students.

The text of this book is enhanced by Dr Hardie's own accomplished drawings, and additional thanks are due to Professor Hugh de Wardener and Dr Dudley Gotla for kindly allowing us to reproduce the Chungkai theatre posters. Mention must also be made of those members of the Museum staff who have been responsible for the book, notably Dr Christopher Dowling and Mrs Janet Mihell. Any publication involves a great deal of work, and long hours have been spent editing the text, checking facts, and reading proofs. The result is a book which will hold its place in the literature of the Second World War.

Alan Borg, Director
Imperial War Museum
July 1983

Introduction

By the summer of 1942, barely six months after the outbreak of the war in the Far East, the seemingly invincible Japanese armies had overrun the Philippines, Malaya, Burma and the Dutch East Indies. In order to improve their land communications in South East Asia and reduce their dependence upon the long and vulnerable sea route to Rangoon round the Malayan peninsula, the Japanese Imperial Headquarters in Tokyo decided to revive a project which had been mooted as early as 1885 – that of building a railway to link Ban Pong in Thailand and Thanbyuzayat in Burma. The engineering difficulties were formidable since the line had to be cut through 260 miles of rugged mountains and monsoon jungle in a region with one of the most unhealthy climates in the world. It was planned to complete the railway by the end of 1943, a date which was later brought forward by several months.

The Japanese had at their disposal a vast and, in their eyes, expendable labour force in the tens of thousands of Allied prisoners of war who had fallen into their hands. Some 61,000 British, Dutch, Australians and Americans were employed on the railway. In addition the Japanese impressed enormous numbers of Tamil, Chinese and Burmese labourers. The Allied prisoners were drawn mainly from Changi camp on Singapore Island but also from camps in Malaya, Java and Sumatra. They were transported to Burma and Thailand packed like cattle in the holds of freighters and in railway trucks, a nightmarish journey which was frequently followed by a long and exhausting march. Men already enfeebled by months of cramped confinement on a starvation diet and equipped with little more than hand tools were forced to work under savage pressure for up to sixteen hours a day, sometimes in ceaseless rain. Their boots wore out, they had practically no bedding and their clothes were soon reduced to rags. The primitive huts and tents in which they lived swarmed with insects and were often awash with floodwater and sewage. More than 16,000 died during the construction and subsequent maintenance of the railway, an average of one victim for every 28 yards of track. But for the skill, ingenuity and devotion of the Allied medical officers and orderlies the death toll would have been even higher. In appalling conditions, using surgical instruments improvised out of scrap metal and with totally inadequate supplies of drugs and dressings, they fought to stem the ravages of beriberi, cholera, malaria, tropical ulcers, dysentery and other diseases.

Robert Hardie, a medical officer serving with the Federated Malay States Volunteer Force, became a prisoner of war when Singapore capitulated to the Japanese on 15 February 1942. After several months in Changi he was sent to Thailand, where he spent over three years in various camps and base hospitals on the Burma-Siam railway. Throughout this harrowing period he managed to keep a detailed record of his experiences, which he wrote on army message forms and concealed inside a thermos flask. Diaries were forbidden by the Japanese and the penalties for being found with one were severe. When in 1944 searches became more frequent Hardie buried his notes in the cemetery at Chungkai camp, recovering them after the Japanese surrender. He transcribed the text virtually word for word on his return to the United Kingdom at the end of 1945 and, it appears, then destroyed the original tattered and fragile sheets. In 1971–1972, during his last illness, he reread the diary and added some explanatory notes, the majority of which have been included here.

Apart from minor stylistic changes, the removal of repetitious matter and the insertion of chapter headings the diary is published as it was written forty years ago. It gives a vivid picture of the hardships, monotony and humiliations of life in the squalid and overcrowded camps which marked the course of what has only too aptly been named the 'railway of death'. As Hardie was the first to admit, he did not suffer as badly as those in other groups, notably the members of the ill-fated 'F' Force, a mere 55 per cent of whom survived their ordeal. 'Many people,' he wrote on 11 September 1945 in a letter to his mother, 'had a far worse time than I did – I was really very lucky, being mostly in biggish camps. The small ones, run by inhospitable savages, were often fiendish.' The only source of hope and comfort for the prisoners who toiled on the railway, besides the irregular and much delayed arrival of mail and Red Cross parcels, was news of the progress of the war obtained by means of secret radio sets, whose operators – men of exceptional bravery – faced almost certain death if they were caught. These news bulletins, to which there are a number of veiled references in the diary, were of incalculable importance in keeping up morale.

The Allied medical officers on the railway faced a daunting task, which not only taxed their professional abilities to the full but called for diplomacy, resourcefulness and also chicanery of a high order. The Japanese were ruthlessly determined that the railway should be completed on time, whatever the cost in human lives. They regarded sickness as a crime and suspected that the camp hospitals harboured scores of able-bodied prisoners who were dodging work. Like his colleagues, Hardie found himself involved in a running battle with the Japanese authorities to secure vital medical supplies, to improve the diet and accommodation of hospital patients, to prevent desperately sick men being driven out to work and to contain the spread of disease. He had to contend not only with the indifference, unpredictability and incompetence of the Japanese but also, as the diary reveals, with a certain amount of selfishness and apathy on the part of his fellow prisoners of war. Hardie himself emerges from these pages as a cultivated, objective, scrupulous and sensitive observer, whose delight in nature was a major sustaining influence during the darkest days of his captivity. Those who knew him at the time speak of his excellence as a doctor, his innate courtesy, his breadth of learning, his high principles, his concern for others and his quiet courage, which was an inspiration to colleagues and patients alike. A gifted artist, he made a number of studies of plants and insects using a child's paintbox, which he bought in Thailand, and colours derived from natural pigments. A small sketchbook which he started at the beginning of 1943 has also happily survived. Some of the sketches from this, and other drawings done on scraps of paper, he later reworked in pen and ink.

I have tried as far as possible to identify the 250 or so people mentioned in the diary, whose names, not surprisingly in the circumstances, Hardie sometimes misspells – 'Lee' for Lea, 'Outram' for Owtram, 'Reid' for Read and so on. I have corrected these where I am certain of the identity of the individual referred to. In the course of verifying names I accumulated a good deal of biographical material relating to the period covered by the diary; as it seemed that this information might be of interest to readers, particularly to survivors of the railway, it has been incorporated in the index. Additional details will be gratefully received. The spelling of camps and stations on the Burma–Siam railway presents a special problem. They were written phonetically and many different forms exist. To avoid possible confusion I have in some cases altered the spellings used by Robert Hardie to bring them into line with more commonly accepted variants.

One of the pleasures of editing the diary has been the contact it has given me with Robert Hardie's relatives and friends. I am greatly indebted to Elspeth Hardie for her enthusiastic help and encouragement; also to the author's sister, Margaret, and his former partner in Malaya, Dr Ian Mackintosh. But for the efforts of Jack Masefield and the distinguished New Zealand surgeon Max Pemberton, the diary might never have been published. My colleagues Roderick Suddaby, Philip Reed and Janet Mihell all made valuable contributions in different ways. Thanks are also due to the many people who kindly supplied information about themselves and racked their brains to recall details of others. They are acknowledged at the end of the book.

Christopher Dowling
Keeper of the Department of Museum Services

Robert Stevenson Hardie

A Personal Note by Elspeth Hardie

Robert Hardie and I were married in Kuala Lumpur, Malaya, early in 1949 a few years after the experiences described in this diary, but we had known each other for a long time. We had met again briefly in Edinburgh when he was repatriated and I was on leave from Germany, but at that time it was difficult for returned prisoners of war to adjust to life in Britain and to talk of their experiences. Bob, like others, wanted to get back to Malaya as soon as possible to the work that he had known before and the friends who had shared his experiences. During his next leave in 1948 he was able again to enjoy meeting people, walking in the hills and fishing in the lochs and streams of Scotland. This love of fishing and the countryside he had absorbed in his youth from his father and from his uncle R. P. Hardie, who remained his companion on fishing and golfing holidays until Bob left for Malaya. The Scot who wants to see the world enjoys and appreciates his own country even more than those who never leave it.

Bob told me that all his life he had wanted to travel – at Oxford when studying Classics he had become interested in archaeology, but in those days it was not easy, without money, to participate in archaeological excavations abroad. When he graduated he passed high enough in the Civil Service examination to enter the Indian Civil Service which appealed to him. Unfortunately he was dissuaded from this and therefore entered the Home Civil Service, but this did not suit him and after three years he decided to study medicine with the thought that he might go as a doctor to India or the Far East. He never regretted this decision – a hard one to take, with five more years to study. He was lucky at the conclusion of his houseman's job to hear, through a friend, that there was a vacancy in a Scottish medical practice in Kuala Lumpur. In 1937 he left for Malaya.

He loved the life there – the work interested him, he made many friends amongst the planters and the business and professional community, many of them fellow Scots. The country fascinated him: he studied the geology, the plants and the birds and enjoyed walks in the hills and picnics by the rivers. He sketched, played the piano, played golf and worked hard. He travelled on leave to Sumatra, Java, Bali and Cambodia and visited Ankor Wat. He planned to visit Kashmir but then war came to Europe. In 1941 he had not been very well and as home leave was impossible Bob went to Australia and New Zealand, where he fished and climbed and enjoyed the climate and scenery. He was in New Zealand when the Japanese entered the war and as he was a medical officer in the Federated Malay States Volunteer Force he was ordered to return in Malaya. He had offered and been accepted to serve with the New Zealand forces because of the difficulty of returning, but by chance a troop ship was sailing to Australia and from there he flew to Singapore. Four weeks later Singapore fell and he was taken prisoner.

I have often been asked how three and a half years as a prisoner affected Bob and it is hard to answer. The impression that is left with me is that he was a very easy person to live with since for him nothing could ever be as bad as the experiences he had endured. He was tolerant, understanding and kind, but prepared to stick up for what he thought was right. There was also something special about his friends who had been fellow prisoners. They knew each other so well and knew what each had overcome and I think this led to lasting friendships.

We returned from Malaya in 1951 and Bob took a diploma in Public Health and worked in Argyll and finally Berwickshire as Medical Officer of Health. After retiring early from Local Government in 1964, he set off again, this time to the West Indies as Medical Officer of Health under the Ministry of Overseas Development to give of his experience to another country going through the change from colonial status to independence. He felt he wanted to repay in some way the great happiness he had enjoyed in Malaya. When finally we retired in 1967 to Scotland, which Bob had always loved deeply, he enjoyed gardening, bird-watching and hill climbing and returned to his old interest of archaeology. Robert Hardie was a person interested in every aspect of life, working with concentration on whatever concerned him. He could share his classical interests with our daughter Alison and his interest in medicine and in nature with me. He kept up with many friends from Oxford and Malayan days and despite or because of his experiences in Siam he was able to enjoy life to the full.

This book will serve as a tribute to the medical staff who helped so many in the prisoner of war camps in Siam.

I thank Dr Christopher Dowling for his kindness to me and for the great trouble he and his staff have taken in every detail of the publication.

Singapore

Singapore

I did not begin to keep a regular, or fairly regular, diary until some months after becoming a prisoner, so that I can only write in general terms of the first few months. Singapore capitulated on 15 February 1942. In July, by which time I was in a POW camp at Ban Pong in Siam, I wrote a few pages about what I saw from the time I arrived in Singapore (by air from Australia) on 13 January onwards; and the first dated entry on the tattered and grubby sheets which I have managed to preserve through many Japanese searches and other vicissitudes is 1 August 1942.

I landed, then, at Singapore on 13 January after an uneventful flight from Batavia. It was about midday when, with curtains over the windows of the flying boat – 'so that,' the steward said, 'you won't see the defences of Singapore' – we flew over the Rhio Archipelago, and began to lose height as we came down towards the flying boat harbour. We sat silent, perhaps rather apprehensive, wondering whether we should hear the stammer of machine guns if Japanese aircraft were about. But nothing unusual happened: down we came on a wide sweep, the engines idling, the flaps down – and then the sudden hissing crash as the boat settled on the water. The doorway was thrown open, light streamed in, and with it the familiar stink of Singapore waterfront and the warm humid air. As we went ashore in the launch, a heavy rainstorm drifted over us and eerily in the middle of it came the wail, rising and falling and rising again, of the air raid warning.

When we reached the shore we were hustled into damp and mosquito-haunted timber and turf air raid shelters, but before long, as not much seemed to be happening, we made our way into the airport building. There we saw Mr and Lady Diana Duff Cooper, attended by a strong posse of the Colonial Secretariat, heading for another aircraft which was to take them away from Singapore. With them was Alex Newboult,[1] who was able to tell me that Margaret[2] was all right, and already in Singapore. From the airport, an Imperial Airways car took us to the Raffles Hotel where we were lucky to get beds – six in a room. There I got on to the Colonial Secretariat by telephone, and was able to speak to Margaret and arrange to see her that afternoon. As I came back to the hotel, I ran into John Daly and Jim Mitchell, who had just reached Singapore with their field ambulance and were on their way to the Sultan of Trengganu's istana[3] near Katong. I joined them there next day, but only for a few days, when I was sent as medical officer to the composite Federated Malay States Volunteer Force 'depot' battalion, which had been collected

[1] Later Sir Alexander Newboult, Chief Secretary, Federation of Malaya.
[2] RSH's sister, who, at his invitation, had gone out to Malaya at the end of 1938.
[3] A residence used by the sultan of this unfederated state on his rare visits to Singapore.

at St Patrick's School. There an attempt was being made to draft useful volunteers to other units as liaison officers, to weed out the sick and unfit and to sort out efficient units for active service. There was a good deal of confusion and lack of clear policy or system. But quite a number of men became attached to the RAF, the RNVR and to other regiments on the island and the mainland, particularly those which had come as part of the 18th Division not many days before and were much in need of liaison officers who knew their way about. The residue of the FMSVF were then moved out to Telok Paku at the extreme eastern end of the island, on shore defence, and I went with them. During the previous few days I had been able to get into Singapore once or twice in the evening and had seen Margaret in her temporary quarters, with Carline Reid and Henrietta du Boulay, in Orchard Road; one evening in particular I remember, when Charles Seed, Pat Madge, Tony Churchill and I had a picnic supper there with the three girls.

Each day the Japanese bombers came over and dropped their loads on the island with no interference from fighters – there were now practically no fighters left on the island – and little, it seemed, from anti-aircraft fire. But one day as I watched from St Patrick's School a sudden heavy black smudge high in the sky over Kallang showed where a Japanese bomber had exploded on a direct hit.

At Telok Paku I was kept fairly busy, seeing sick men, arranging for hospital and dental cases and their transport, and drawing up a plan for collecting posts for wounded behind that sector of the shore of which the FMSVF had taken over the defence. Our quarters were in the Harbour Board bungalows close by, and from there, day after day, we saw the distant Japanese bomber formations pursuing their steady course over Singapore. A few Hurricanes, recent arrivals we heard, seemed quite ineffective. The dawns and sunsets seen from the bungalow on the shore were very fine – misty pinks and opals thrown across the clear pale blue of the dawn sky, and at sunset brilliant glowing expanses of crimson, orange, purple and green; over in the south, on the horizon, dense billowing black smoke coiling and spreading upwards from the *Empress of Asia*[1] burning with occasional flashes of red flame.

Shortly after the beginning of February, I think – by which time Margaret, with Harold Desch's help, had got away to my great relief on a British India ship for India – I was transferred back from Telok Paku to the 3rd Volunteer Field Ambulance,[2] then occupying Nan Yang Girls' School on the Bukit Timah Road north of Singapore and running a small hospital there. Our mess was in the library building. Ian Mackintosh and I slept in the gallery, the rest in small rooms downstairs.

The hospital was kept full with ill men and minor surgical cases: we were not equipped for major surgery. Bombers came over, but few bombs fell in our vicinity and little time was spent in shelters. Our Asiatic orderlies spent too much time and energy dashing to their slit trenches at every possible alarm,

<hr />

[1] A troopship carrying elements of the 18th Division, which was attacked and set on fire by Japanese bombers as it approached Singapore on 5 February 1942. Most of the men were rescued but much-needed arms and equipment were lost.

[2] Note by RSH. This was my original unit before I went on leave to Australia in August 1941. The commanding officer was Paddy West (wounded and in hospital when I reached Singapore). J. Coutts Milne was in acting command. Other medical officers were Ian Mackintosh and Jim Mitchell.

a proceeding which was hardly soothing for the large number of patients we had who could not leave their beds and had to lie gazing up at the roof tiles, which were all that separated them from the sky. But on the whole these Malay, Indian and Chinese orderlies and NCOs did well – remarkably, when one remembers that they had left their families behind in the north in places now in Japanese hands. On reflection one can see that it was unreasonable to demand that these men should retreat down the peninsula with the British troops, leaving their families behind. But in the end little harm was done, for they were disbanded before the capitulation in order that they might reassume civilian clothing and make their way back to their homes. And practically all of them did so successfully.

The 'medical inspection room', where we did small dressings, was on the north side of the north-west wing, facing the Japanese positions a few miles away – the Japanese had successfully landed on the north-west coast shortly after the beginning of the month. The Japanese had some mortars and, not long after my arrival, they began firing over us into the town. The shells went whispering overhead but each one sounded as if it were coming in at the window. The hospital was never hit, but a few shells fell close enough to sound dangerous and the bangs of the guns maintained a certain tension. Lots of Japanese aeroplanes cruised overhead but only once did any number of bombs fall anywhere near us, and they were several hundred yards off. One was much nearer; it came down in the sun flashing like a 40lb salmon – and failed to burst.

Ambulance drivers, messengers, despatch riders brought in all sorts of rumours – that the Japanese were advancing rapidly; that they were at Bukit Timah racecourse three miles away; that the Americans had landed at Penang and Port Dickson in the rear of the Japanese and were advancing rapidly rolling them up from behind; that there was fighting on the Causeway again; that the Japanese had been driven out of Bukit Timah and several miles back; and so on. We heard, too, that two shipments of Hurricanes had been landed at Singapore, and sure enough a few days later we saw three or four in the air, but they seemed to have no speed and we heard later that they had not been at all successful.

It had become clear that the Japanese were closing in and that we should soon have to go back into Singapore. One evening we found an Australian unit lining the north side of a slightly sunken road behind to the south of us; they told us that they were there as a precaution while they cleared away a dump of stores slightly further back. They did not know what the position was further forward but their proceedings suggested that we were rather exposed. The night was very quiet, the silence only occasionally broken by a rifle shot or a burst of automatic fire. To the west as well as the north there was a glare in the sky – presumably burning dumps. One didn't sleep well, and was beginning to feel a sort of heavy hopelessness about the situation.

Next morning there was a lot of traffic hurrying south into Singapore; a big dump a few hundred yards north of us began to burn with billowing clouds of black smoke, and the roar and gleam of fire could be seen through the trees. Mortar shells began to go over us, and some burst not very far away. Our orderlies spent practically all their time now under cover, and our walking wounded – a good many had simply left in the night and presumably made their way back to the town – were dodging about too. Those unable to move

17

looked pretty unhappy. Coutts Milne went in to the medical base to suggest that we should be brought back. Colonel Cornelius replied with the consoling suggestion that, as we were probably nearly cut off, we had better stay where we were. However, the petrol dump fire seemed to be coming nearer through the trees and finally Cornelius sanctioned our evacuation. Coutts Milne arranged with a motor ambulance convoy to clear us and in the afternoon we got on with the job of loading 180 or so men into the ambulances.

Our last few hours at Nan Yang were hectic. Japanese aircraft circled unmolested overhead and did some sporadic but ineffective machine-gunning. I actually saw one single-seater coming low over the trees from which the pilot, leaning out, pitched a hand grenade down on the Bofors anti-aircraft gun site. There were a lot of Bofors guns round us in the early afternoon, barking continuously, but we saw no hits: by the late afternoon they had all gone back. Finally all the wounded were put into ambulances and, after a last look at the school with its scarlet-flowering flame of the forest trees brilliant in the sun against the dark clouds of smoke to the north, we got into our cars and made our way back through the northern suburbs of Singapore, where we passed a number of anti-tank guns ready manned and pointing up the roads along which we had come.

As we neared the centre of the town the converging traffic became heavier; civilians were plodding inwards along the road. In the centre of the town – we were directed first to the Raffles Institute, later to the St Joseph's Institute – we saw the crowds of 'masterless men' (in khaki) who had retreated, many probably without orders, without arms or equipment, and were wandering about, uncontrolled and demoralised, seeking shelter and food where they could. It was a melancholy and terribly depressing sight. It was 11 February, and Singapore was only too clearly doomed.

We were not, of course, in contact with the troops who were actually fighting but it was quite obvious from the number of disorganised bands of weaponless and undisciplined men that control had broken down, at least at the centre. We knew by this time that no attempt had been made to organise defences on the north side of the island until far too late, and again and again we heard of retirements against orders, refusals to counter attack and so on. So weak was the defence that I believe that not only was the main Japanese landing quickly established, but even the feint landing at another point met with practically no opposition and established itself without difficulty. Some self-respecting and resolute units continued to fight well, but it was evident that in general morale was low, and Wavell's last blistering order two or three days before capitulation made painful reading.[1]

It has become clear to us since the capitulation how inadequate had been the grasp before and during the war of the main strategic considerations for

---

[1] On 10 February 1942, during his last visit to Singapore, Wavell dictated a note to Percival which contained the gist of a strongly worded telegram from Churchill. Percival issued this as an order of the day. Part of it read as follows: 'It will be disgraceful if we yield our boasted Fortress of Singapore to inferior forces. There must be no thought of sparing the troops or civil population and no mercy must be shown to weakness in any shape or form. Commanders and senior officers must lead their troops and if necessary die with them. There must be no question or thought of surrender. Every unit must fight it out to the end in close contact with the enemy.' When this order was handed to the senior Australian medical officer for promulgation to Australian Army Medical Corps units he tore it into small pieces.

the defence of Malaya. The only built defences were on the south coast of the island – and these were incomplete. It is easy to be wise after the event, but surely the limitation of fixed defences to the south side of the island involved a high degree of blindness to the strategic situation in the Malaya–Siam–Indo-China area. How could a hostile naval force approach Singapore from the south so long as the Malay peninsula, Sumatra, Java and Borneo, with airfields, were in our hands? It was of course the defection of Indo-China and Siam which enabled Japan to roll up our land positions: but when the Japanese actually attacked Malaya, the preparation of defences in the north had hardly been begun and there appeared to be little concerted planning between RAF and Army. During the retreat down the peninsula there was time to prepare for the defence of the north side of Singapore Island, but this appears to have been entirely neglected until hopelessly too late. By that time morale was low, and victory was a walk-over for the Japanese . . .

After our return to the middle of the town of Singapore, which was crowded with guns, transport, unit HQs, hospitals, ambulances and troops organised and unorganised, we joined forces with Colonel Malcolm's 1st Casualty Clearing Station[1] hospital in St Joseph's Institute, a big, dusty and flimsy school building, but with useful blast-walls, wisely put up along the lower arcades by the Brothers before the war. Our last days there were hectic, nervous and weary. We got few serious wounded, so far as I remember, except casualties brought in from close by from shell-fire or bombs, but had a lot of lesser injuries and a number of cases of shell-shock, and all degrees of nervous reaction from hysteria and prostration to mild 'shaking-up'. There was a fair amount of work to do, and it was more or less continuous. Rather foolishly we slept upstairs but John Daly, a gunner in the last war, maintained that the Japanese artillery was negligible and that the fresh air to be enjoyed in a room giving on to an arcaded verandah looking north was worth any small risk. One night, however, a shell burst in the roof directly over us and we promptly moved down to a verandah on the ground floor, facing in the opposite direction. A number of shells hit the building, but no damage was done to any patient or staff. Some of the shells failed to explode.

Two or three days before the capitulation, a civilian Chinese ambulance driver was brought in with minor abrasions, having collided with a truck driven by an Indian. I walked back with him to his car, which was near at hand, and we found it out of action. It was already being looted by disorganised Indian troops. So I saw him back to his local emergency ambulance station, about half a mile away. The streets were deserted except for a few prowling Indian soldiers, all on the north side of the streets – for the shells, though there were not many, were coming from the north. At the entrance to the Motor Ambulance School Section, which was protected with blast-walls, was a pathetic crowd of Indians and Chinese; among them I saw the amah whom Margaret had had in Kuala Lumpur, the wife of Tom Grieve's 'boy'. There was nothing I could do except give her some money and wish her luck.

Then, on the evening of Sunday 15 February, an uncanny silence fell over the town. It was a relief from the racket of Bofors, field guns and bursting

---

[1] Note by RSH. Of the medical officers in Colonel Malcolm's CCS I remember best Eric Cruickshank. I met him again when he was Dean of Medicine at the University of the West Indies, Kingston, Jamaica, in 1964–1967.

shells, and aeroplanes. But it was a tragic silence. It was difficult to grasp what had happened but the fact was plain enough. Singapore had surrendered, unconditionally.

Inside our hospital it made little difference to our activity. The supply of water remained scanty and of doubtful purity but it did not cease; we continued to live off our ration stores and were ordered to maintain the blackout; and we continued to look after our casualties.

Japanese bombers and fighters swept triumphantly low over our heads during the following days. A huge Japanese army flag was hoisted over the towering Cathay building, and a smaller one on the mast on the Fortress hill. Civilians began to move cautiously about the streets, in which Japanese staff cars and transport were the only traffic. Here and there squat Japanese sentries were posted. Industrious Indians and Chinese brought cigarettes round to the hospital – obviously army supplies – and sold them for high prices.

We occasionally heard firing in the distance – presumably Japanese liquidating the Kempeitai's[1] victims – but there was no disorder so far as we could see. A day or two after the surrender, the Japanese held a victory parade of tanks through the town. The procession passed close to our building; it was a painful spectacle. Parties of British, Australian, Gurkha and Indian troops appeared in the streets, clearing up fallen rubble, burnt-out cars and crippled transport under Japanese direction. Coutts Milne, who had somehow got himself a Japanese armband, was able to go out and about a little, and kept us informed of what was happening outside – the marching of the troops out to the barrack area at Changi, 13 or 14 miles away, and the arrangements being made to transfer the hospitals also to that area.

One morning about ten there passed in front of the hospital a pitiful procession – the civilians (European) marching out on foot to the civil prison at Changi where they were to be confined. It was a painful sight – most of the men elderly, some spare and erect, a few very stout and sagging, they filed past carrying their belongings or pushing or pulling them on improvised barrows and hand carts, themselves dressed in soiled and crumpled white, or shabby torn khaki. In the hot sun, humiliated, dirty and weary, they staggered past. Two or three dilapidated buses carried the women and children. The population lining the streets, but not in great numbers, seemed to feel the depression, and looked on in silence.

Towards the end of February the transport of the wounded to an extemporised hospital in the Roberts Barracks at Changi was carried out, and we went too, almost last of the hospital staffs. It was Colonel Glyn White of the Australian Army Medical Corps who organised the move, the RAMC command being apparently unequal to the task. I marched part of the way through streets in which many shops and houses had suffered severely. Here and there terrible stenches from the ruins told their own tale. After a few miles I was picked up by Coutts Milne in a car, and we did the rest of the journey in style.

The barrack area of Changi, to which all the prisoners of war except the Indian native troops were sent after the capitulation, is a fairly extensive tract of country at the eastern extremity of Singapore Island. It consists of undulating irregular ridges, with a good sprinkling of trees. There are several big groups

20   [1] The infamous Japanese military police organisation.

of large barrack buildings, and elsewhere many good-sized bungalows. Owing to the way in which the ground has been used, many of the big barrack blocks and many of the bungalows, especially those at the eastern extremity where the ground slopes fairly sharply to the beach, have magnificent views to the east and north. To the north and north-east lies Johore, across the quite narrow Johore Strait, which is the channel to the naval base.

The British Hospital was in the Roberts Barracks, the Australian in the Selarang Barracks. On our arrival we went to the Roberts Barracks to see if we could be of use. Sick and wounded were arriving constantly, before accommodation was ready. The chaos was indescribable. There appeared to be little organising ability among the higher medical ranks. It was clear, however, that there were more than enough medical officers of the RAMC available, so after one night in the barracks – my recollection is of flustered senior officers wandering about bleating ineffectually, junior officers endeavouring to reconcile conflicting instructions, and of great difficulties in getting other ranks to stick to the heavy jobs of cleaning out the barrack rooms and carting beds up the stairs – I rejoined the FMSVF officers, 75 of whom were living in a fairly large bungalow. It was pretty crowded, there was no water (it had to be brought up from a well in a small valley three or four hundred yards away) and the only food was rice, supplemented by a small amount of extras which had been brought in by various units. This was inadequate to supply more than flavouring for the rice. After a week or two we had to evacuate this bungalow and moved down to a row of small houses fairly close at hand. I had a persistent eruption of pemphigus blisters on my arm at this time, never serious, but a great nuisance. I saw a lot of Harold Desch at this period. He lived a few doors along the row, and we used to walk around the curving roads in the neighbourhood in the evenings. There were fine views to the east and north over the beaches, and one high point gave a magnificent view also to the west and the sunset.

Mitchell, Turner and I looked after the FMSVF personnel (other ranks) while Ian Mackintosh and Ross McPherson looked after the officers. It was not very strenuous as we were able to send practically all the bad cases along to the hospital; but there were regular sick parades to be done, and matters of sanitation and hygiene around the barracks to be attended to. We had regular but exiguous supplies of drugs, as the main stocks were rightly kept for the hospital. The main shortage was of vitamins to supplement the obviously very deficient diet. We got no green vegetables or fruit; the rice, poor in quality, was polished; there was only very occasionally a trace of meat. Vitamin B deficiency symptoms appeared within three months of the capitulation, showing that the diet during that time was almost totally lacking in that particular vitamin.

One spent one's free time going for short walks, playing chess, gossiping or reading. At first I spent a good deal of time daily in washing clothes and sweeping out the room but as soap became less and less procurable one reconciled oneself to less clothing, less often washed. It was not long before schemes were prepared for instructional courses in languages,[1] in wireless telephony, shorthand and so on. These were sporadic and unofficial at first, but later a more elaborate curriculum was arranged, there being plenty of qualified

[1] Note by RSH. I attended a German class run by a teacher in the Education Department. I forget his name. He died in captivity in another group in Siam.

teachers in the forces in our area. Webb, Chaplain to the FMSVF, did very good work organising evening discussions and lectures.

Contact with other areas – our area was Southern area and there were in addition the Hospital area and the Australian area – was limited, but very small numbers were permitted to go from one to another at stated times, under escort. I succeeded in getting over to the Australian area once or twice and made contact with Leslie Greener, an Australian journalist and artist whom I had known in Kuala Lumpur and whose wife and friends I had met in Sydney (and very kind and hospitable they were). With him lived Murray Griffin, the official Australian war artist, who was doing very interesting sketches of camp life. It was a refreshing change to spend an hour or two with them.

Outline of a typical day:

6.30am	FMSVF sick parade (with Mitchell or Turner).
7.15am	Breakfast. Porridge (of ground and half-roasted rice). Sometimes a trace of sugar, occasionally a sip of tinned milk. Tea. Occasionally a slice of rice bread.
8–9am	Sweeping, washing clothes and self; shaving.
9.30am	Medical inspection room dressings. Barrack visit – sick and sanitation. If back early, chess, reading and writing.
12 noon	Lunch. Rice, perhaps with a little ghee or rissole (rice, rice-bread, trace of meat possibly). Afternoon classes, reading, sleeping, darning, sewing, chess.
5.00pm	Evening meal. Rice; thin tinned veg or fruit gravy. Afterwards, walk and talk with Harold. Occasionally poker with Ian, John Daly, Henry Mills and others.
8.30pm	Lights out.

Uneventful, tedious days, wondering, wondering. There were endless rumours, some helpful, some depressing. As people recovered from the first dejection, lectures were organised on contemporary events – The Career of the Battleship *Prince of Wales* by Claude Aylwin, Royal Marines, a survivor; The Malayan Campaign, by General Sir Lewis Heath. One came to realise only too well the lack of foresight and imagination, the absence of determination and of organisation, the shirking and the failures that led to the surrender of 65,000 men to about 50,000.[1] I had no first-hand knowledge of the cardinal errors and failures; but I could see and verify small items in the colossal mass of error, selfishness, obstinacy, incompetence and indifference which led to the disaster. Training and morale were inadequate; the troops felt that too much was demanded of them; their officers sometimes failed in resolution and leadership. 'There was no air support,' was the constant cry. But the army should have done better even without it.

I won't expatiate further on this topic, however. The British army did not show up well in the campaign, nor did the behaviour of a number of men and officers in the first months of imprisonment do much to increase one's admiration of human nature. On the other hand there were many admirable

---

[1] In fact the balance of forces was even more unflattering to the British. The strength of the Singapore garrison at the beginning of February 1942 after the evacuation of the mainland is officially estimated at 85,000, of whom some 15,000 were base or administrative troops. During the campaign the Japanese deployed three divisions numbering approximately 35,000 men.

examples of patience, cheerfulness among the sick, of public service without much thanks among volunteer cooks and teachers; and of good temper and forbearance generally.

One remembers moments of pleasure: evening walks along the stretch of road above the beach, looking over to the green islands of Johore with their fishing craft and huts along the shore; sunsets, some of them indescribably brilliant, viewed from the top of the watertank hill; the rare and wonderful curries that made possible the consumption of a phenomenal quantity of rice; evening conversations with Dane Meads on a slope overlooking the sea; brilliant moonlight – and it is true that one constantly reflects that the same moon is visible to other people very far away; my minute and rather absurd Greek class in an open shed in Changi village, the *ad hoc* chapel of the British Battalion[1]; visits to Quaife (an elderly estate practitioner from near Kuala Lumpur, roped in to the army at the last moment), to Coutts Milne and the 'anti-malarial unit' in Changi village; an afternoon with Greener and Griffin in the Australian area; the drawing class which I attended with Harry Malet, at which we decided we were the only people in it who could draw at all; plays got up by various units – *The Chocolate Soldier* on Temple Hill, a review in the 'theatre' at Changi village. But, underlying everything, the heavy feeling of monotony, futility, waiting and wondering.

From time to time working parties were made up and left the camp to go to Kranji, to Blakang Mati, to the Race Course, to River Valley Road camp. First Mitchell went off to Blakang Mati, then Turner to the Race Course. I was not detailed until late June, and then, with Ian Mackintosh and an RAMC hospital group, for a 'mainland' or 'up-country' party. We did not know what our destination was to be, and speculation covered every possibility – Johore, Tanjong Malim, Cameron Highlands, Tanjong Pau, Bangkok, Chiengmai, Saigon – we could get no information except that we were to go north into the peninsula by train. We were up before dawn on 26 June, the day we were to leave Changi for the mainland. A final run over the baggage, a hasty cup of tea and piece of bread, hurried farewells and then off to the hospital, with baggage and a wheeled stretcher pushed by John Daly and Henry Mills, kindly coming along to give us a send-off. At the hospital Ian and I met the rest of the hospital party which was accompanying the working party draft, Majors Read and Black, Captains Hatreed, Davies and Hort and Captain Arkush the dentist. Our baggage was loaded into lorries and we packed in ourselves. A wave to John and Henry and we were off at the tail of the convoy, on our way to Singapore.

At the station platform a goods train, consisting entirely of covered wagons with a sliding door on each side, was waiting for us. The non-personal baggage and heavier articles of personal baggage were put in a separate van. Carrying our own stuff, we were divided into groups of 25 or 26, and each group was allotted a single closed van. The baggage went in first and almost completely covered the floor, although it was in theory piled round the sides and ends. In we piled too; it was a tight fit, but we did not know at all how long the journey was to last and were not unduly dismayed.

These iron wagons were our residence for the next four nights and days.

[1] Formed in December 1941 from the remnants of the 1st Leicestershires and 2nd East Surreys after both battalions had suffered heavy losses.

Discomfort, heat, thirst and fatigue made it a nightmare after the first twenty-four hours.

Twice a day the train stopped at some pre-arranged station where food was ready – rice and a small quantity of soup or stew. Drinking water was not provided but sometimes it was possible to buy fruit (bananas and pineapples) and coffee. At Prai, I remember, where we halted just before dawn and saw Penang Hill in the early light, wreathed in clouds, we were actually given real bread and almost a third of a tin of salmon each. This was an unexpected and unique treat. It was the last real bread I was to have for a long time.

Inside the trucks as we travelled discomfort was considerable. Only the people in the middle of the truck, opposite the open sliding doors, got any fresh air; the draught to some extent stirred up the air in the other half of the closed van by blowing in as the train moved; but the front half was desperately hot during daylight. The iron walls and roof became too hot to touch when the sun shone, and mostly it did shine, though I remember some rainstorms. At night the iron became cool, but it then 'sweated' and one tended to become chilled in contact with it. It was impossible to sleep properly in that welter of legs, boots, bodies, angular baggage, knobbly packs and unyielding suitcases. If one dozed, one's head fell back against the rattling and jolting iron wall of the truck and one was knocked awake again.

Not only was drinking water short: only at the rarest intervals could one get even a splatter of water for washing oneself, let alone one's clothes. Sweating, cramped and crowded in these trucks, unshaven, bleary-eyed and dirty, we soon presented a shocking appearance; and not merely appearance, but smell.

Still on we trundled northward. We stopped at Kuala Lumpur in the early morning, few but Japanese in the station. This was almost the only spot where any sanitary conveniences existed. As we moved out of the station again Ian was able to see his house standing above the railway line. It was closed, except for an upstairs window, and looked undamaged. Ipoh was reached that evening, Butterworth and Prai next morning – that was where we had the bread and salmon. The following morning we were in Siam. At some station there at which we stopped I remember the station master coming out with a great platter of fried eggs and distributing them as fast as he could, free, to an appreciative crowd. Quite a lot of fruit, too, was thrown into our trucks at various points by generous Indians or Siamese.

At dawn after the fourth night we crossed a big river bridge at Ratburi; the view westwards up-river to a huge triple pagoda on a hill blazing in the yellow early morning light was unforgettably striking. At about midday, the train halted at a station, Ban Pong, and we were ordered to get out. Apparently we had reached our destination.

We had no very clear idea where in Siam we were, but for the moment we did not much care. Shouldering our kit, leaving behind what we could not carry in the hope that it would be brought on later by transport (most of it was), we staggered out of the station and lined up on the road outside. The Japanese had to satisfy themselves that we were all present. After endless waiting, endless shouting and argument, count and recount, they appeared satisfied and we marched off through the shabby little town. The open wooden shop houses seemed to have fair stocks of goods, we noticed, and we looked with covetous eyes at piles of fruit. As we came out of the town, the road

24

deteriorated. Squalid pigs, cats and ducks nosed about at the sides; the houses seemed untidy and dilapidated, the inhabitants on the whole unbeautiful and dirty. Vultures tore obscenely with their beaks at something nameless in the long grass at the roadside. Newly constructed huts of bamboo and palm leaf (attap) appeared on both sides with mud, disorder, decaying refuse, mangy dogs, transport vehicles of various sorts, and many dwarfish untidy Japanese soldiers. More mud and more new huts, and British troops moving among them – evidently the party which had preceded ours to the 'mainland' two or three days before. Then a sort of gate in the fence on our right, a small piece of open muddy ground with the Japanese guards' hut on one side near the entrance, and beyond long lines of low bamboo and attap huts closely ranged together – our future home, evidently.

Ban Pong

Ban Pong

July 1942

Our camp is an area about 250 yards square, between the railway and the road which run eastwards from Ban Pong in the direction of Bangkok. It is surrounded by a rather flimsy bamboo fence, beyond which to east and west are banana plantations and fruit trees. Most of the camp area is occupied by the attap huts in which we live. Except on the west side, where there is a little open strip with a few sugar palms and coarse grass, the ground is black earth, which, when there is any rain, becomes a swamp of sticky but very slippery black mud. The huts themselves are flimsy structures of bamboo, thatched with attap; at ground level their width is about eight metres, and the sloping roofs come down on each side to almost two feet above the ground. Down the middle of each hut, which is about 80 yards long, is a central passageway about two metres wide, and down each side platforms of rough planks extending back to within a foot or two of the lower edge of the roof. Between the huts is a narrow space about two metres wide. Inside the hut each of us has a section of platform about four feet wide and eight feet from front to back. It is darkish inside, as the light comes in only from under the eaves, and from the openings at each end and in the middle of the hut. One puts one's kit at the back of one's space, and can use the bamboos of the hut frame, and strings stretched between them, for clothes and other belongings. Dust filters down all the time from the roof; in the woodwork of the platform lurks an endless army of bugs, while ants are everywhere. Myriads of mosquitoes hide in the darkness of the roof. The 'hospital' is exactly the same, and one does one's round crouching or kneeling on the platform beside the patients.

The latrines lie in a line along the bottom ends of the huts, at a distance of three or four yards. They are only two or three feet deep, of an utterly unhygienic open bamboo construction on top; and there are not nearly enough of them. The result is that the bottom ends of the huts are nearly uninhabitable owing to the stench and the clouds of flies and bluebottles. But the huts are so crowded that the bottom ends cannot be evacuated. Again and again we have asked the Japanese to give us a little timber to construct proper latrines, dug 10–12 feet deep according to British army pattern. But they will not even supply the raw wood.

There is no place to wash. If one can get some water, one must carry out one's ablutions standing on the narrow path between the huts. But merely getting water is extremely difficult. In the first place there is no well or source of water in the camp at all. The nearest well is 300–400 yards along the road, and in order to reach it one has to go out of the camp, past the Japanese guard house at the entrance. One can only do this in organised parties, which are limited to small numbers, so that the total amount of water that can be brought into the camp is necessarily small. In addition, there is an acute shortage of containers. A bucket used for bringing water from the well could be used again if there were any tank into which it could be emptied; but at present no such reservoirs exist. Most of the fit men are out working all day and sometimes they get a bathe in a ditch or pond while they are out. But it is absolutely out of the question for them to wash when they get back in the evening after their day's work. There has not been a sufficient number of fit men in the camp to fetch water for them. Even if there were, there are not enough containers for carrying the water and there is no space to store it till the evening. So dirt and skin diseases are becoming more and more serious.

Furthermore, malaria has begun. The Japanese alleged when we came (we raised the question at once) that there was no malaria in Ban Pong. But now, presumably in consequence of all the digging and construction going on in the neighbourhood, and the arrival of our men (a good number of whom must be carriers, having got malaria during the campaign perhaps and not having been completely cured) fresh cases are beginning to occur. We have asked the Japs again and again (a) for Romanowski stains, to examine blood films. Ian has brought his microscope with him, fortunately, since our medical command in Changi would not give us one when we left. (b) for an adequate supply of quinine. We only brought a small quantity from Changi – why so small when they had literally rooms full of it, I don't know. (c) for mosquito nets (only about 50 per cent of the men have nets) and (d) for permission to undertake anti-malarial measures round the camp. But the Japanese are totally indifferent and do nothing: when pressed they indicate that they do not believe we are having cases of malaria. We tell them there will be a serious epidemic. It does not produce a flicker of interest.

Cooking arrangements for this camp are also very bad. The cookhouse is close to the well, about 400 yards away along the road outside the camp. It is ludicrously ill-provided with cooking utensils and the absence of containers is aggravated by the long distance the food has to be carried into the camp – this arrangement also ensures that all food is practically cold before it is issued. The cookhouse itself is primitive, tumbledown and dirty. There is no satisfactory arrangement for the disposal of swill, and the place is infested with flies. Supervision is extremely difficult owing to the distance from our camp and the fact that the cookhouse is not enclosed by a fence.

It is true that our rations are adequate to support life if one is well to start with. We get a reasonable quantity of rice, an ounce or two of meat daily and a fair amount of vegetable, though not of very good quality. But owing to the container shortage it is impossible to make anything out of the rations except stew. So every day it is rice and stew, morning, midday and evening: and that is tepid or cold owing to the delays in bringing it from the cookhouse. People ill in hospital do not have an easy time. It is very difficult to make any special dishes for people whose insides are disordered. Rice and green vegetables aggravate dysentery; tepid stew is unattractive to people with malaria or other infections involving fever. We do what we can to buy eggs and a little tinned milk, but it is extremely difficult to get even a fraction of what we need.

It is a squalid, monotonous, depressing and humiliating existence. How long is it going on?

The country is flat round about so far as we can see, the earth black and rich, with fine fruit trees – bananas, pomelos, mangoes, limes and sapodillas – round the native houses, and great open areas of padi land. This seems to be some sort of centre for railway construction and the rumour is that a new railway is to branch off here for Moulmein in Burma. Some preliminary work has been done about two or three miles along the railway to the east: a number of sidings have been made, and there is another prisoner camp alongside occupied by about 600 men who came up a day or two before us. We saw them when we arrived in this village, but they have since been moved out to the camp along the railway.

We shall see in due course what we are here to do. Meanwhile we continue to exist, in an atmosphere of futility and depression.

Occasionally there is a break. Once in a while a party is arranged to march under Japanese guard through the town and out to the river bank above it; there for about an hour one can bathe and wash one's clothes and feel more at large. Such glimpses of the outside world are extraordinarily heartening. The men who go out daily on working parties are perhaps less liable to depression for this reason than are we, who have to stay in the squalid camp. I know I have greatly enjoyed the two days I have been out with a working party. I had nothing medical to do, and merely strolled or sat about in the area where the party was working. But it was a pleasure to be able to look round over a wide stretch of open padi, with here and there groups of trees. It gave at least an illusion of freedom.

1 August 1942

Last night I had an extraordinarily vivid dream that I was walking about the lawns round the ruined cathedral at Dunkeld. It was summertime and there were flowerbeds with great banks of flowers . . . I shall see them again I hope, perhaps before very long.

2 August 1942

Sunday morning. Reveille goes at the usual time, 7.30am. This is 'Tokyo' time, 5.30am sun time in this part of the world when it is still dark with just a faint glimmer in the east. Lying in our unlighted attap sheds in which, when all is silent at dusk and dawn you can hear the shrill hum of countless mosquitoes, stiff from an uncomfortable night on wooden boards, we rouse ourselves and grope around, perhaps with the help of an occasional flash from a precious electric torch, for damp shorts, shirt, and socks and shoes. Then one staggers out into the dim dawn for the morning roll-call, held on the road outside the camp. If there has been rain – there was a little last night – the paths between the huts and the road, being of beaten alluvial mud, became unbelievably slippery and cake on one's feet. 1,800 men, a tousled, unwashed, crumpled, smelly and disagreeable crowd, flounder past the Japanese guardhouse – we all have to salute humbly as we go past – through the narrow gateway and out on to the road where we sort ourselves out in our sections, in fours.

At 8 o'clock a simian Japanese NCO with very short legs and an assistant with a big sheaf of papers come down the line and receive from each section a report of numbers, for example, 'Twenty on parade, four sick, six on duty, total thirty.' The follower takes it all down and, reaching the end of the column, is plunged in calculation. If all is well we are dismissed, stumble back to our huts, and can then shave and make our apology for a wash from the exiguous quantity of water we have stored up in a canvas bucket. Then breakfast, at present broken rice-sweepings boiled to a mush ('porridge') plus some vegetable and meat stew (rather sour) and a cup of tepid smoky tea. Today, after reveille, as we have done on previous Sundays, we heard the distant bells of the Italian Mission, a sound almost unbearably poignant, coming to us from the free outer world; it seems to accentuate our helplessness and futility.

The diesel-drawn passenger trains that drum past the back of the camp, just on the other side of the fence, with their comfortable coaches and their Siamese passengers in colourful clothes, also underline for us our captivity. So the days drag on.

5 August 1942

After over a month of off-putting by the Japanese, supplies of fruit (chiefly bananas), ducks' eggs and sweet biscuits are now being admitted to the camp for individual purchase. As we are paid at the rate of 25 cents a day – NCOs 15 cents, other ranks 10 cents – we have a small amount of cash for such purchases. The eggs have to be already hard-boiled as we have no means of cooking them; they are 5 cents each, and the bananas (10 to 15 to a bunch) 5 cents a bunch. This makes a considerable difference to our life, for on our present rations we are always hungry. Our diet has deteriorated since we came here and were it not for these extra purchases it is possible that we should be beginning to suffer again from the oedema and neuritis which was so prevalent in Changi two to three months after the capitulation. We rather wonder if the Indian Army colonel who is our senior officer makes sufficiently strong representations to the Japanese. He appears to think that as we surrendered unconditionally we have no right to expect anything, and that anything we do get is a favour of the Japanese.[1]

The Japanese are certainly not easy to deal with. When pressed for certain ameliorations of our condition – milk for dysentery patients or better general rations for everyone – they do not hesitate to lie, saying they have no milk. We know this to be untrue for working parties at the station have handled large numbers of cases; the sentries at the guardhouse are often seen consuming tins of it and one of our medical officers who went across to the Japanese hospital found a group of officers drinking it iced – one even threw away a whole glass because it was not cold enough. They also claim that our rations are better than those of the Japanese themselves, which is simply untrue, for the Japanese cookhouse is close to ours and our men know what the Japanese get – some of them act as servants in the Japanese quarters.

6 August 1942

Today Mitchell of the FMSVF died in hospital. He was a quiet individual, who never looked very robust. He had had a spell in Changi hospital with bacillary

---

[1] Note by RSH. This may be unfair: one was inclined, under the conditions that prevailed, to put the worst construction on anything.

dysentery, but had been out and convalescent for three to four weeks before coming to Thailand. I had rejected him for the 'mainland' party when I went through the lists at Changi; but pressure was put upon me by Brigade to pass as many people as possible. It was pointed out that working parties in Singapore were well fed and well treated, not hard worked; and it was suggested that a mainland party might expect as much, or better; while the food in Changi itself was pretty poor and prospects not good. So, as Mitchell seemed to be convalescing well, I marked him 'unfit at present but likely to do well given good conditions'; and on the supposition that the conditions on the mainland were likely to be better than those prevailing in Changi he was included in the mainland party. I feel now, of course, that I ought to have been more positive that he should not come; but it was difficult to be very positive in such circumstances.

7 August 1942

Mitchell was buried this morning. In blazing sun, wheeling the coffin on a ramshackle handcart, we crossed the open space to the camp entrance past the lounging Japanese guards and turned along the road. I noticed one or two Siamese stand at attention as the little procession went by. We continued past the muddy cookhouse area, along a path over some overgrown waste ground, to a quiet corner among thickets of scrub and creeper, where five parallel ridges of dusty earth mark the graves of those who have so far died at this camp. In that untended spot, under the fierce sun, the short service was held, the Last Post and the Reveille blown. Mitchell was married and had two children – it will be long before they hear this news, I am afraid, and I can imagine no sadder or more futile death.

12 August 1942

The Twelfth. I suppose there will this year be little of the activity usually associated with this day in London and Scotland . . .

These last two days I have been out on working parties – on the former up to a small Japanese camp on a common just outside Kanburi, I think, a fine open breezy site on sandy soil, with a view of smallish rough limestone hills to north and west of the town. Kanburi (Kanchanaburi) is about 30 miles north-west of here. It was very refreshing to get away from the confinement of Ban Pong: this was only my third trip outside the camp since our arrival five weeks ago. It was an interesting if jolty run by lorry over the rich padi plain, very wet, with its irrigation canals, its patches of bamboo and fruit trees, its banana plantations and dense patches of thick scrub in unplanted corners. As one approached Kanburi, which like Ban Pong is on the River Mekong, the groups of limestone hills rose out of the flat alluvial plain. It was exhilarating just to see them. I and the rest of the party had a good midday meal there – the Japanese troops' food which they (they have no connexion with the prisoner of war camps' organisation) quite amiably gave us – well-cooked rice with some good vegetable and a trace of pork, as well as a good deal of a sort of flat biscuit-pancake which they seem to use a lot. Yesterday I was out with a working party at the new junction station. Little work was done, but one was able to buy bananas and pineapples.

There seems a possibility that, as a result of further representations from our senior officers backed up by the medical officers' reports, something may be done to improve our conditions. We have protested against (i) the bare adequacy of our rations, in particular the shortage of protein (ii) the absence of any washing facilities at all (iii) inactivity over malaria (drugs, nets, ground survey and anti-larval measures) and (iv) the insanitary latrines. There is a chance that new latrines will be authorised. The feeding and cookhouse question remains acute. Apart from the arrangement by which our food is cooked a quarter of a mile away, the rations generally have deteriorated. There is certainly some pilfering in the cookhouse. Yesterday a sergeant cook was caught selling some of our exiguous rice and tapioca flour ration to some Siamese. It is almost incredible that people should behave so when their comrades are short of food. But this captivity has revealed that the veneer of decent behaviour is very thin indeed in all ranks, and hunger and craving for variety have worn it off in places.

15 August 1942

We have now been prisoners for six months – 182 days. It has been long enough; and time here in the dirt and discomfort of Ban Pong passes painfully slowly. There are, however, a few minor improvements. The canteen is functioning fairly regularly, and supplies of eggs, bananas and sweet biscuits are on the whole well maintained. But still there has been nothing done about washing facilities, and apart from one or two ampoules of emetine (for amoebic dysentery) there have been no supplies for the hospital, no nets and no word of any action to cope with the malaria danger.

18 August 1942

I am having dengue fever – not a serious matter but a very uncomfortable disease, with severe aching in all the bones, so that it is difficult to find any comfortable position to lie in. The Japanese camp commandant has, we hear, been removed to the Japanese hospital with a sharp attack of malaria. Lying wearily in this dark hut all day, I have thought with longing of the luxury of minor illnesses at home – cool clean sheets, cool drinks – all the comforts so strikingly absent here where bedding is always damp, dirty and smells of sweat, and the food primitive and monotonous.

21 August 1942

Yesterday was the last day of my dengue fever, very uncomfortable with the usual final flare-up of temperature and aching. Today, beyond feeling flabby, I am all right again. Yesterday morning there was a special ceremony at the early morning roll-call, which was called 20 minutes earlier than usual – in practically complete darkness at the beginning. We were kept standing out there for an entire half-hour till a posse of Japanese officers, including a lieutenant-colonel newly appointed in charge of prisoner camps in Ban Pong, arrived. The lieutenant-colonel made a speech, translated haltingly and obscurely, by an inadequate interpreter. The lieutenant-colonel forgot his words and there was an awkward pause while one of his underlings hunted up a copy of his remarks, after which he went on a bit faster. The gist of it was that he was glad, he said, to have been appointed to look after our camps. He had heard that we were working well and that our health was good and he undertook to give us 'the best treatment from a great nation, if possible' – if we continued to work hard and cooperate with the New Order. The whole ceremony, held at dawn and long-drawn-out, before we had had anything to eat, was extraordinarily unimpressive, and even farcical. (I myself was not feeling too well and many others must have been worse, but if one missed these roll-calls one got no pay for the day.) It is, however, something that we have a senior Japanese officer in charge of us. It means at least that we are not so completely under the powers of vindictive and quite unenlightened underlings. Perhaps the conditions of our existence may be expected to improve a little. Perhaps not.

Yesterday the sky was amazingly fine, a deeper, clearer blue than usual; great white cloud masses, snow-white on the sun and with beautiful shadows, towered into the sky, brilliant and sparkling.

There are rumours of great developments in the war but we hear nothing certain. Is there a second front? What are the Russians really doing? The Japanese themselves seem to say what we have captured some of the Solomon Islands from them. Perhaps this is the beginning of an important development.

23 August 1942

In the last day or two a new Japanese commandant has taken over. Perhaps he may be more helpful. For things have reached a serious pitch. The hospital now has practically no drugs – nothing except a little magnesium sulphate for treating the rampant skin diseases. 'Treatment' in the hospital is virtually nil.

Colonel Williamson says that some timber recently dumped inside the camps is for washing-places.

25 August 1942

The planks referred to above are being used to build a new office for the Japanese administration. The only concession as regards washing is that bathing parties are taken along to the river daily if wanted. This makes a pleasant outing; but owing to the large numbers of men whom the Japanese take each day for working parties, the number of people free to go on the bathing parties is extremely small. Men who can possibly work, work; for the sick get no pay.

3 September 1942

Today is the third anniversary of the outbreak of war, and we now enter the fourth year, in which, Churchill told us, we should begin to feel our strength and use it. It seems that we have begun to push in the New Guinea region, and what we hear from there – we occasionally see a *Bangkok Times* – seems favourable. There are rumours as well of lightning attacks and great advances; but the equanimity of the Japanese lends no support to this optimism.

The hospital conditions remain desperate. The number of cases of skin disease is going up rapidly. There is almost no gauze and only a handful of bandage; and no lotions except a little copper sulphate, a little biniodide and common salt. It is painful to see men with great areas of oozing eczema and big septic spots without adequate covering, let alone medication. There is a lot of scabies, but no sulphur; a great deal of tinea, and only a little salicylic acid to treat it with.

Working parties continue. The total absence of washing facilities in the camp remains a crying deficiency, and is of course the primary cause of the gross amount of skin disease. In hospital it is practically impossible to wash bodies or clothes and so infection is reapplied and spread. Food has improved slightly. By paying a daily 5 cents into a common fund, we have been able to get a little variety: pork fat for frying; a little extra sugar; and some curry. It makes a tremendous difference.

10 September 1942

This monotonous life continues. Our roll-call parades at dawn and dusk are now held inside the camp, on the muddy space between the huts and the western fence. Here we stand twice a day for a quarter to half an hour while the local mosquitoes (malarial mosquitoes are most active at dawn and dusk) attack us. New cases of malaria and dengue keep coming in. Skin diseases multiply daily and the means of treating them are at vanishing point.

A semi-official intimation has come from the Japanese that an 'anti-malarial party' may be called for to go up-river – 100 kilometres, they say – to 'supervise' anti-malarial work. I am to go in charge of it, if it goes. Volunteers have been called for, but the only ones so far are mostly other ranks who have been in India and have seen camp hygiene work being carried out by Indians. None of them knows anything, really, about it, and all would be quite unsuitable for supervisory work. A number are just bad hats who have been in trouble so often in this camp that they spring at any chance of moving somewhere else.

12 September 1942

The Japanese have announced that about the end of this month we are all to be moved up to the neighbourhood of Kanburi. It seems possible that there will be some anti-malarial measures where we are going; but evidently the 100 kilometre up-country party has been dropped.

The rainy weather continues; the camp this morning was a frightful quagmire.

There is good news from New Guinea.[1]

18 September 1942

I am getting very depressed with my hospital cases. The shortages of dressings and drugs make treatment as understood in civilised countries impossible. Against the huge areas of infected spots and pemphigoid eruptions, against huge deep ulcers (these indicate a lack of resistance to infection due to deficient

36   [1] Note by RSH. We now had a secret radio set working in the camp.

diet) and scratches and cuts gone septic, the available wisps of gauze and surviving fragments of grubby bandage are quite useless. How the men who suffer from these horrible conditions keep cheerful and sane beats me. The hospital has over a hundred patients. Occasionally the Japanese give us a packet of gauze or half a bottle of some lotion; of course, it goes nowhere. But by having a 'hospital' the Japanese save face. They close their eyes (is it complete indifference, incompetence or policy?) to the fact that the hospital is a mere pretence. We recently saw an announcement in the *Bangkok Times* that the Red Cross authorities were satisfied with the treatment being given to prisoners in Thailand. Of course no Red Cross authority has ever been here.

We have been playing a little bridge in the evening, huddled round a dim lamp on our sleeping platform – Ian Mackintosh, Duncan Black, Colonel Owtram and myself. Yesterday I bid and made a small slam – a triumph for a beginner.

The camp is again a quagmire; this morning's roll-call in rain and darkness was a desolate affair. We come back to a stone-cold breakfast now, for the food is brought to the huts *before* roll-call and left there during the half hour or so we stand outside being counted.

Kanburi

Kanburi

2 October 1942

There has been a gap of ten days since my last entry. On 23 September Read told me that I was to accompany 100 men of No. 3 Battalion who were going up to somewhere near Kanburi for railway work. Next day – another drenching morning – we paraded an hour after dawn, and everything got thoroughly soaked before we started. We travelled in open lorries up to the 'Aerodrome' camp on the common at Kanburi – that was as far as I had ever been in this direction. But we did not stop. We went on, turned left into the walled town of Kanburi and went right through down to the river bank beyond. 'Walled town' is a rather grandiloquent description. Tumbledown battlemented brick walls enclose, probably very incompletely, an area the dimensions of which, in this through trip, I was not able to see. Within this area are scattered buildings, trees, grass and a good deal of overgrown untidiness of one sort or another – hovels, hen runs, corrugated iron sheds, abandoned orchards. The distance between the squat whitewashed gateways was no more than two hundred yards, so the walls probably represent the outlines of a fort rather than of a walled town. On the river side of the fort is the main street, with shops of one, two or three storeys on each side. Our road down to the bank cut across it at its south end, and we only had a glimpse of the street running northwards for what seemed quite a considerable distance.

At the river bank were moored a large number of big barges and small motor boats, of characteristic appearance. Our party loaded into two barges, each of which was to be towed by a small launch. Marsh[1] and I travelled in the launch which towed the leading barge. We chugged out into the wide river and saw that our embarking point was in fact just below the junction of two rivers, one, rather swift, coming down from the north straight past the town, the other, wider and much slower, coming in towards us from the west. We headed obliquely across the main stream losing 'ground' as the current was strong and turbid – this was the rainy season and the river was high – and then worked up and turned west into the wider and slower stream which came in on the far side. This river was about 150 yards wide, with heavy vegetation, mostly feathery bamboo, on the left side and open ground extending back on the right. Behind the bamboo on the left and stretching round northwards in front, lay a range of broken and jagged limestone hills, covered with bushes and scrubby bamboo. Up we went, keeping mostly fairly close to the bank to avoid the central current, past vast rafts of lashed bamboo poles with little attap shelters on top where the pilots live during their down-

---

[1] Note by RSH. 'Hajji' Marsh, an engineer from Socfin, Kuala Lumpur, a tower of calmness and strength at all times.

stream journey, other rafts of teak logs and small native houseboats moored along the banks.

Three or four kilometres up, the limestone hills on the left came closer to the bank; and on the other side, too, a high limestone ridge fell sharply to the water's edge. Just short of this, where a tall bamboo pylon with the Japanese army flag rose out of the green bamboo (the stems of which are 30–40 feet long), we came in to the steep earth bank, disembarked at a ramshackle bamboo landing stage and climbed up on to the level ground. There we found a small camp occupied by some Japanese troops (engineering units) and a detachment of 60 British prisoners under Mundie and McLean of the Argyll and Sutherlands, who had been here for a day or two. Our party went into tents (20 men each, extremely crowded) alongside the tents of the earlier party. Marsh, Peacock and I and the other two or three officers of our party were accommodated for that night in a corner of a bamboo and attap hut occupied by the Japanese troops.

Next day we got a separate hut built – sides and sleeping platforms of bamboo, roof of canvas. It is small, and stiflingly hot so long as the sun is shining, but we have been able to put a bench of bamboo under a fairly shady tree close by at the edge of the clearing, and it is there that I am sitting writing these notes. The Japanese sergeant who is in charge of us allowed me to have a small hospital hut built, sufficient to accommodate half a dozen sick men and the two orderlies (Norris and Weir) whom I have with me. This gives me a place where I can hold sick parades and have people under observation if necessary. Not that I really have any medical supplies. I have a pair of scissors, a pair of dressing forceps, a couple of square feet of gauze and two or three yards of bandage; in the way of drugs, a little quinine, some magnesium sulphate and some salt, and some flavine lotion. But fortunately there is no serious sickness at present.

The men are being sent out in working parties chiefly to clear the railway trace and to make a cutting through the shoulder of limestone that comes right to the water's edge a little upstream from here. We also send a small party to clear a space for the big new camp which is to be constructed here. This is pretty slow work as the ground is fairly heavily overgrown with creepers, bushes and banana trees; and as the railway engineers want as many men as they can get for their trace and clearing and working at the cutting, they take all the fit men and only leave a handful available for the clearing of the camp site.

A civilian Japanese interpreter, who is attached to our Japanese sergeant, tells me that all the Japanese troops here are taking a quinine tablet a day (their tablets are about 3 grains). He says that actually there is no malaria here, but up-river a lot. A Japanese doctor, he says, prospected the area the summer before the war began.

This little camp, surrounded by high vegetation on all sides, lies on a narrow track which runs down towards Kanburi. There are a few native houses not far away where one can buy odds and ends of food – bananas, papayas and so forth; in particular banana fritters, cooked hot as you wait over a charcoal stove, and a sweetmeat made of boiled raw sugar and roast peanuts – very good stuff. As I am not at all busy, I have time to wander about, and there is no difficulty about getting away from the camp area along the various paths that run into the jungle. There are semi-derelict areas of all kinds of fruit cultivation – papaya trees, pomegranates, guavas, bananas, custard apples, mango trees, trailing pumpkin plants and cucumbers, castor oil bushes, wild passion fruit creeper and so on. Except where bamboo thickets monopolise the ground, there is a riot of vegetation, in which it is very easy to lose one's way. A short distance down the track towards Kanburi one comes to the area where the large new camp is to be. Only a small area is cleared so far but the ground is more open, and free from bamboo. It has obviously been cultivated in the past but extravagant weed growths have crept in and the whole place is a derelict wilderness with a few fine trees. Some Siamese, apparently in the employ of the Nips, are pottering about with bamboo poles and seem to be about to start with the building of one hut in the area so far cleared.

In the other direction (north-west) the path almost at once obliquely crosses the railway trace, which comes in from the starboard quarter on its way to the point where the cutting has been started. Beyond this open space, the path plunges through some thick bamboo and emerges into a more open piece of ground, well shaded by big trees – mangoes and tamarinds – among which are some fairly substantial native huts, raised on piles and with verandas. Here, beside the path, is a table on which fruit is laid out for sale: some coarse bananas and some bunches of the small bright yellow thin-skinned variety. The men call them 'monkey' bananas for some reason – they are like the golden banana, the pisang emas, of Malaya. There is also a charcoal stove, behind which sits a woman peeling and slicing bananas, dipping them in a bowl of batter and dropping them into a curved flat frying plate half full of simmering and sizzling oil. When cooked, the fritter is hot, sweet, crisp and very good. One gets eight or ten for 5 cents.

Pausing to pick up a bundle wrapped in a banana leaf, one goes on a little and emerges into a wide open sunny space with the steep limestone ridge on the right and in front. In the middle of the open space is a wide, cement-floored, open-sided building in which almost 40 children are at school. They are all small, I don't suppose any are over nine or ten, the girls in little white blouses and charming tightly wound little blue sarong-skirts, the boys in khaki-green shirts and shorts. The singsong repetitive chant of the children learning their lessons sounds very pleasant and cheerful. As we walk past the sound stops; the teacher looks at us a little doubtfully, the children mostly with beaming smiles, although the younger ones look solemn and rather awe-struck. Half right, close under the overgrown limestone rocks, is a brick platform under a dilapidated but decorative wooden roof; on it sits in deep shade a big plaster figure of Buddha, dark and cobwebby, with a few withered flowers and strips of cloth at his feet, and here and there a rough earthenware vase with a few charred joss-sticks in it.

Having crossed the clearing, one plunges again into the undergrowth and bamboo, recrosses the pegged line of the railway as it reaches the beginning of the cutting, and finds oneself standing on the slope of the limestone ridge as it falls sharply into the river. Where the path scrambles round the steep face, the view is very fine both down and up the river. Downstream extends a broad straight reach of wide smooth water, with feathery bamboo on each side, the darker green of big mango trees rising here and there. In the other direction, one is looking up a very wide flat valley, an unbroken floor of green of slightly varying shades, with blue cloud shadows drifting over it. Well back on each side are low green hills, dimmer and bluer as they close in far up

the valley ahead. At one's feet the river, emerging from behind a bluff a little higher up on the other bank, swings round in an exhilarating steady sweep. The railway, after breaking through this cutting, will launch out on to this wide valley floor and run far up into these dim distances.

There are said to be five or six camps already working up there, clearing the trace of the line; the river must be navigable for 70 or 80 miles above us. No doubt it is these camps that the barges and launches which go up and down the river are engaged in supplying. The Japanese are evidently pushing on the railway construction as fast as possible. The flora and fauna of this region are very interesting and varied. There are beautiful butterflies, some very big ones with black narrow forewings more than six inches from tip to tip, and brilliant canary-yellow hind wings, veined and spotted with black; a smaller species has brown-black wings with a purple sheen, very striking in the sunlight. Others are white, yellow, russet and blue, spotted and barred. A particularly common one has sooty black wings and a brilliant crimson body. Then there are innumerable birds – kites, eagles, hawks, falcons; babblers (a fine jay-like bird with a white head and brown body); hoopoes, woodpeckers, drongoes ('king-crows'), shamas, bulbuls; and the brilliant azure-blue jay (Indian roller), as well as innumerable kingfishers.

Three days ago Basil Peacock (the senior officer of our party), CSM Lawrey (a tin-miner from Malaya) and I had a trip into the town of Kanburi with the Japanese interpreter and Lieutenant Gota. We went down by launch with a detachment of Nip soldiers going in for a day's leave. On landing we went to the police station inside the walled area, and had to wait about there for a bit while the Japanese apparently conferred with the Siamese police. After this we went to the main shopping street where we looked for, and found, soap, buckets, washing basins, toothpaste, cigarettes, notebooks and so forth

– things needed in the camp and not, of course, supplied by the Nips, even for the hospital. We ended up at a large general and grocery store, where an attractive Siamese girl, having sold us some brown sugar, insisted on presenting all three of us with a big bunch of the large sweet bananas which are more expensive than the others.

The Japanese interpreter, rather to our relief, asked us if we were hungry, and when we said we were – it was now about 2pm – took us to a Chinese eating house and stood us an excellent lunch, a sort of risotto with a fried egg, slivers of pork and cucumber, well flavoured, satisfying and unusual, which we greatly enjoyed, as we did also a big glass of hot coffee, richly sweetened with tinned milk and sugar.[1] Then back to the general store where we sat about till it was time for our boat to go back to camp. During this waiting period, the shop was greatly frequented by all and sundry, and we talked to many of them – a local 'doctor' who runs a 'clinic' in the town (he had no English); a schoolteacher or two; the district nurse (sister of the girl in the shop – she spoke a few words of English); and so on; besides a lot of nondescripts who seemed amiable but were incomprehensible; and the usual handful standing on the pavement and simply staring. Japanese soldiers frequently came in to buy odds and ends.

It was altogether a most enjoyable day, though we were not sorry (desultory conversation in broken English is exhausting if it is prolonged) when the time came to go down to the river bank with all our purchases. The Nipponese soldiers turned up, in good order except for one man who was extremely drunk. He gave a classical performance of drunkenness all the world over, talking loud and fast, rolling heavily against his neighbours in the boat, roaring with causeless laughter, suddenly shouting out military commands, and unsteadily getting to his feet and saluting solemnly towards the shore.

6 October 1942

Work is being pushed on at the new camp area. One hut is partly roofed, and some of our men are being moved down into it today. We are told that about a thousand men are coming to this camp from Ban Pong in about a week. At the present rate there will be nothing like enough accommodation for them. We have kept insisting to Chotani, the Japanese sergeant, that it is important to get latrines dug before these men arrive, but he is only interested in the huts, and we can get neither picks nor spades for digging – nor, of course, men to dig: they all have to work on clearing or building. There is, however, much more space available in this new camp, so the huts will proba-

---

[1] Note by RSH. I omitted an episode in Kanburi on this occasion, one which I thought perhaps the Japanese might not like recorded if they found my diary. Basil Peacock refers to it in his book [*Prisoner on the Kwai*] though I hardly recognise myself there as a 'Scots doctor' with a Harry Lauder accent. After our lunch Gota left us for a bit in charge of a Nip corporal (or was he a Korean?) who thereupon made it clear that he wanted to visit a house towards the northerly end of the Kanburi street. Basil and I – I can't remember if Lawrey was there too, probably he was – followed him and he went into what was evidently a Japanese army brothel (if there had been any doubt about this the corporal's leers and gestures would have made it plain enough). We were not invited inside, fortunately. I remember saying to Basil that this was the lowest point to which we had yet sunk as prisoners – waiting outside a brothel for our guard to emerge. This he did in due course, not evidently very pleased with his entertainment but not so angry as to take it out on us. We went back to the shop and continued to wait for Lieutenant Gota and the party of Nips.

bly be better spaced – there are more than 10 yards between the two lines so far laid out – and it will be possible to site the latrines at a reasonable distance from the huts.

20 October 1942

A lot has happened since my last entry. The main body came up from Ban Pong some days ago – about 900 men. They were told before they left Ban Pong (from which they marched to here in three days, with very inadequate food, water and shelter on the way) that the camp here was 'practically ready' for them. Actually, of course, owing to the action of the Nips in our advance party camp (we were supposed to be building the new camp) in demanding all or practically all the fit men for the railway work every day, the new camp consisted only of two huts which, crammed to the doors, could not hold more than 500 men. There were no latrines, no cookhouses and no arrangements for water supply though Basil Peacock and I had repeatedly made representations that some preparations should be made in these matters.

We have been in the camp a week now and have got something done to make the place more sanitary. But the men are packed like sardines in their huts – each man literally has a space about a foot wide (by 6 to 7 feet front to back) on the ramshackle bamboo platform. Sleep and cleanliness are almost impossible for them.

Now we hear that several thousand more men are coming up from Singapore, and huts are to be built for them. One wonders for what proportion of these thousands huts will in fact be ready.

Sufficient latrines have now been dug. A new cookhouse is not yet completed; and cooking for the camp of nearly 1,000 men is being done over picnic fires – not an easy task. Water suitable for cooking and drinking is utterly inadequate: our only water source is the river, which is extremely muddy. Not only is sterilisation necessary if the water is to be drunk – and we are painfully short of containers for boiling it and have little chlorination material – but it is essential to remove the vast amount of suspended grit in the water before using it for cooking. But so far we have only one filter, a wooden box about the size of a chest of drawers, filled according to the plan devised by Nobusawa.[1] This plan consists in putting palm leaves at the *bottom*, then sand, and, on top, stones and then bigger stones. The palm leaves at the bottom have rotted, and in addition to having practically no filtering action, the box delivers water that stinks of rotting attap. We have, however, got permission to construct a box to be filled according to our own ideas.

There is no sort of fence round the camp as yet, and one can still slip out for walks in the surrounding country when one has free time. I have not had much recently, since I am pretty busy with the hospital here, which I am running with Duncan Black. We have for accommodation only the little hut which I originally had built in the small advance party camp, and an end of one of the finished huts. We can only accommodate 20 or 30 hospital cases at present – between 200 and 300 men who can't work owing to sickness (mostly malaria and skin troubles) have to stay in their sleeping places. I spend

[1] Note by RSH. On a famous occasion the Japanese interpreter referred to him as 'our so-called doctor'.

a great amount of time trying to get medical supplies out of the Japanese – as difficult as wringing blood from stones. Nobusawa professes to have almost no supplies for us and we have practically no dressings for our skin cases. A tin or two of quinine tablets, half a bottle of spirit, one or two bandages, three washing bowls, a couple of buckets and a bar of soap constitute the 'hospital equipment' in a camp of nearly a thousand men.

The Japanese are building their offices and sleeping quarters with squared timber but they won't even give us enough planking to make a lid for the filter. When the main party came up and it was necessary for 300–400 men to sleep on the ground (most in the open) the Japanese issued a number of them with grass or bamboo strip mats to lie on. Now they have collected all these mats again to use them for walls and partitions in their own offices. In the same way in the small advance party camp, because we had only a 6-gallon container to boil water or tea for drinking for all of us, they gave us, under pressure, a 40-gallon iron drum which seemed to solve our problem. But next day it was taken from the cookhouse by the Japanese sergeant, who used it to make a heater for water for his bath.

Withholding as they do virtually all medical supplies and materials for promoting hygiene, they yet complain continuously of the large numbers of sick, and attribute it to our incompetence and 'bad spirit'.

I had a good afternoon's walk a day or two ago with Padre McNeill along the padi flats to the north and up into the limestone hills – exhilarating to get high up on a limestone peak and view the country round for many leagues. We saw many birds – mynahs, woodpeckers, falcons, a jungle cock – and a brilliant electric-green tree-snake with a wicked diamond-shaped head in a thick clump of bamboo.

The party from Ban Pong tell of the flooding of their camp – the whole area was up to 2 feet deep in water, both inside and outside the huts, and over the latrine area. The conditions can barely be imagined; they lived ankle-deep in sewage.

I have had a note from Ian Mackintosh – he did not come up with the main party, as he had dengue when they left. So he stayed behind looking after the 200 or 300 sick in the camp there with two or three other medical officers. A lot of parties from Singapore are coming to Ban Pong, where they stay a night in the flooded camp, and then go on, leaving their worst sick behind. There have been a number of FMS Volunteers in these parties; but they have not come to this camp – they evidently go straight through to camps up-river. They were told by the Japanese in Singapore before they left that they would find a 'fully equipped hospital' at Ban Pong where they could leave their sick. All these parties from Singapore have had the benefit of the stores from the Red Cross ships which unloaded at Singapore in September. They received quite large quantities of bully beef, milk, porridge and cocoa and many have brought a fair amount up with them. Some units hold quite large numbers of cases, which they have managed to bring up as baggage. We who left Singapore before these luxuries arrived feel rather envious. No attempt appears to have been made to send up any share for us.

1 November 1942

The huts in the additional camp area have been completed and occupied by the units newly up from Singapore. They are tightly crowded as usual – $1\frac{1}{2}$ feet per man or so. We have managed to get from the Japanese a 40-gallon drum for boiling the clothes of men with scabies and other skin diseases, and a start was made today with the hospital skin cases. Water supplies have improved with the installation of a pump-filter. Cooking is settling down, and life is generally more tolerable – except in regard to medical supplies. The units from Singapore, however, have brought a certain amount with them, which has helped a little. The 'isolation hospital', a bamboo and attap hut in the far corner of the camp area among trees and bamboo, is almost finished. It is a long way from the river bank where the cookhouses are and from where all water has to be carried, but it is nicely secluded and out of the way. The present hospital is still merely the end third of one of the huts in the main block; it will have to be kept on when the isolation hospital starts, as the latter will not take more than the sore throats and dysenteries alone.

I have got a small anti-malarial party together, made up of FMSVF officers who have come up with the new units. We have permission[1] to wander over the ground outside the camp area, keeping an eye open for mosquito-breeding in the pools and swampy areas. McCutcheon of Labu Estate is in charge of the party, which is under my general supervision. Smith Laing, also a planter from Negri, is in the party. I met him before the war at a Volunteer training camp in Port Swettenham. He comes from Inverness, McCutcheon from Castle Douglas. The medical officers of the Suffolks (Cayley) and the Cambridgeshires (Longbottom), which constitute the main body of the people newly up from Singapore, seem very competent and agreeable, and have ingenious ideas for concocting therapeutic compounds from substances locally available.

There has been only one death in this camp so far, Cowell (Loyals) who died, of acute yellow atrophy as far as we could see, three days after I had administered some tablets which Nobusawa gave me as 'cough' tablets. Cowell had a fairly severe bronchitis. It looked almost as though these tablets were acutely poisonous; they looked very like – and I thought they were – Dover's powder tablets, which would have been very suitable. One of Cowell's comrades (with whom he was not at all popular) told me that he was always saying that if a man were sick he was much better to ask the Japs for something than to go to our own people. When he got his cough I asked Nobusawa to see him, to convince the 'so-called doctor' that we really needed something for his cough – we had nothing suitable – and he was given three dozen tablets or so. After he had had six (2 three times a day) he seemed rather more drowsy than I should have expected – there is very little opium in our Dover's powders – and I stopped them. He had no more, but next day began to vomit and look jaundiced. He became more and more drowsy and jaundiced and in three days was dead.

I have had one or two more very pleasant afternoon walks in the padi fields and in the limestone hills to the north of the camp, exhilarating scrambles among rocky ridges and peaks which give superb views over the surrounding country. It is pleasant to sit up there in the sun and the breezes and gaze around – it gives one a wonderful sense of freedom to get right away from the camp.

---

[1] Note by RSH. I got a piece of paper from the Nips with some Japanese writing on it which, as I found on the one occasion when we met a Japanese party who were inclined to wonder what we were doing, was quite effective. It evidently explained and authorised one being outside the camp and not on the railway trace.

Hills north of Kanburi camp

8 November 1942

Eight 'battalions' (detachments of 600) have now come up from Singapore via Ban Pong, which they found a nauseating sea of mud and floodwater. Ban Pong is almost entirely a sick camp – the sick left behind by our original detachments, and the sick left en route by these new parties coming up. They have a lot of malaria, dysentery and skin disease. The conditions there are unbelievably squalid – water a foot deep in the hospital huts. Ian and the medical officers with him are having a bad time.

There are signs here that fresh malarial infections are taking place. My anti-malarial party deal with any breeding areas they find and keep looking for new places, but the thick bamboo and scrub make an exhaustive search difficult. There are so many malaria carriers among our men that, if there are suitable anophelines about, further spread is likely.

Under a new arrangement, apparently fixed up with the British government, officers are now given monthly pay. The total amount nominally paid to us varies according to rank. We actually get 70 ticals per month irrespective of rank: the Japanese deduct 45 ticals per month for 'food and accommodation', a small sum (the equivalent of not more than £5 pre-war) but even so a grotesque charge for food which can't on present prices (as ascertained from Siamese) cost the Japanese more than 15 cents per day, and for accommodation which consists merely of a roof and bamboo slats to lie on. The remainder of the monthly pay – except for the 25 cents per day we get in cash – is, the Japs say, being banked for us in a Savings Bank. All officers pay a levy (2 ticals per head per month) to improve the men's messing – a rather niggardly contribution it seems to me. A couple of eggs a day, plus a bunch of bananas ($2 \times 7\frac{1}{2}$ cents plus 10–15 cents) makes a supplement to one's rations which should rule out vitamin deficiencies.

Hospital supplies are still lamentably deficient. Scabies is rife, and we have practically nothing to treat it with – even if we had, the effort would be in vain, with the men sleeping so closely packed and without sufficient supplies of soap to wash either themselves or their clothes. The 40-gallon drum for boiling clothes had no sooner been put into use than it disappeared, no one knows where or by whose agency: it simply vanished in the night.

The 'isolation' building is now in use and is very satisfactory. It is nowhere near big enough to take all the serious sick in the camp, only the sore throats, dysenteries and a few bad malarias. The Japanese at first proposed to put all the sick in a long, exceptionally low and narrow hut which they have just built not far from the isolation hut. It was dark, 100 metres long with doors only at the ends and half way down at the sides, and a narrow passage only a little more than a metre wide down the middle between the sleeping platforms, and that obstructed by the poles supporting the roof, so that a stretcher could not be carried down the passage. Duncan Black and I after great efforts persuaded Colonel Williamson to protest to the Japanese.

At first he was simply told that the Japanese commander had given orders that the hospital hut was to be like all the other huts but, suspecting that this was merely the device of a junior clerk to stifle our protests, we persuaded Skinner our interpreter – a prisoner who speaks Japanese – to speak to Adachi, the Japanese official interpreter; and finally, after a tremendous amount of arguing, we succeeded in getting permission to build a more suitable hospital behind the isolation building. We had to undertake to build the whole thing ourselves: this will mean officers must build it as all the men are used for work on the railway. Work will start at once. If we can carry out our plans, it will make a very suitable hospital, though we shall need more equipment. At present our total 'plant' is ten zinc pails, one rice bucket, seven enamel bowls, two lamps and a 40-gallon drum which I acquired from the Japanese for holding water at the hospital. The day-to-day supplies for the hospital consist of the ordinary rations plus a few eggs. Now and again we get a bar or two of soap. Pycock, our quartermaster, does what he can for us.

A matter on which I have for some time meant to make notes is the prominent part which Federated Malay States and Straits Settlement Volunteers have played in these POW camps. There are quite a number of good officers among the British troops from home, but also a surprising number who do not show much sense of responsibility, and unless forced to do some job simply lie back and contribute nothing to the general welfare. In spite of the fact that there is nothing to prevent them going out at least for walks – and the country round about is very interesting and attractive – too many people spend the day lying on their backs in the huts. But in the camp it is striking how many of the important jobs are held, and not at all badly done, by Volunteers, of whom there are proportionately very few. Tom Watson replaced a British army officer as adjutant of No. 3 Battalion at Ban Pong; Rutty was sergeant i/c cookhouse (an important job); Adams was messing officer; Sandy Currie was officer i/c canteen. Balfour looks after camp sanitation, Shannon after the water supplies; Marsh supervised hut construction.

Up here arrangements are much the same. After Adams went up-country he was replaced by Russell. Working parties inside the camp have been mostly under CSM Lawrey. These jobs refer to a single battalion, with about 60 officers all told available. There is actually only one Volunteer officer not specially employed. In spite of their higher average age (nearly 15 years above that of other officers) the 'whisky swilling planters'[1] are not doing too badly. Outside that battalion there is McCutcheon i/c anti-malarial party – but I got him appointed because he knows all about anti-malarial work, which a home officer could not be expected to understand. Smith Laing, who is attached to the Cambridgeshires, does their canteen work as well as helping in the anti-malarial party.

22 November 1942

In the fortnight since my last entry there have been three leading developments: (i) the arrival of further large numbers from Singapore (ii) the great flood and (iii) the inception of the anti-malarial scheme.

(i) About 4,000 more men have come up from Singapore in parties of from 100 to 700. Of the later parties many are recognised 'Attend Cs', in other words unfit for work, either on account of recent illness or earlier bad histories, or on account of age. There are quite a number of elderly HQ officers. Many of these were so much affected by the rigours of the journey from Singapore to Siam (they were even more crowded than we were) that they have had to be left in Ban Pong. Others have fallen out here; and others are bound to get sick very soon if they go on. The Japanese are entirely indifferent about such cases. One man, just before the party left Singapore, was found to be having diptheria. A strenuous attempt was made to induce the Japanese to allow him to be taken out of the party and another man to be substituted. They refused, and the unfortunate was crammed into a goods truck with 31 other men and in these conditions did the four days and nights journey. The result is that we now have spreading diphtheria here. Davies – working with Ian at Ban Pong – has it, and there are now a few cases in this camp. We have no antitoxin, and hospital accommodation is so strained that proper isolation is almost impossible.[2] Incidentally these parties have brought up good news: we appear to be getting the upper hand in New Guinea and in the Solomons, and the Japanese naval losses seem to be heavy. There is also news of our tremendous success in Libya, which is very cheering.

[1] On 15 January 1942 the *Daily Express* in a stinging editorial placed the blame for the reverses in Malaya on 'a pack of whisky swilling planters and military birds of passage'.
[2] Note by RSH. There were a good many deaths in Chungkai and Wang Lan as a result of the spread of this infection.

(ii) The Great Flood. About ten days ago, after heavy rain here (and presumably more up-country) the main river away behind the camp, which joins 'our' river at Kanburi, overflowed its banks and flooded across country up to and right into the back of our camp. The new hospital building (not yet in occupation) and the isolation building (full) at the north-west corner of the camp were flooded: the water crossed the latrine area along the northern boundary of the camp area and came right up to the huts on that side. The lower ends of these huts were flooded to a depth of a foot or two, and about a third of the total length made uninhabitable. The isolation hospital had to be evacuated and its cases packed into a hastily cleared end of an already congested hut. Our own river, which also rose equally high, flooded half of the cookhouse accommodation on the bank, so that cooking for the whole camp has become extremely difficult. The flooding has put the pump and box filters out of action and we have no means of clearing the river water, which has to be used for cooking, of its silt – and it is like pea soup with the flood. So our food is not only unappetising and reduced to essentials: it is a mass of grit.

Duncan Black pointed out to Colonel Williamson that this would lead to a lot of bowel trouble, and asked him to approach the Japanese with a view to organising a better water supply. But Colonel Williamson solemnly replied that only if Black could say that the use of unfiltered water would result in 'mass deaths' could he ask the Japs to do anything. Duncan was not of course prepared to go to such lengths, so Colonel Williamson said that he did not feel he could approach the Japanese, and we must make the best of the situation. Fortunately someone discovered a cement-lined well in an unflooded area not far away, and we have been able at least to get some clean water for drinking, for the hospital and for some of the cooking. There is nothing like enough for everybody, however. Our food is still extremely gritty and there has been a great increase in the number of cases of diarrhoea. Medical supplies are no better. Lieutenant Saito (Ban Pong Japanese medical officer) has been up; he seems to have some knowledge, speaks reasonably, and it is possible things may improve.

(iii) Anti-malarial work. After the worst of the flood had subsided, leaving water lying in all the hollows in the open and in the bamboo and undergrowth round the camp, I found a lot of anopheline larvae in many of these pools. It became a really urgent matter to get the pools drained, or a severe epidemic was inevitable. I asked McCutcheon to make a comprehensive inspection of the area involved, in collaboration with R. B. Perkins (a planter from Johore and a qualified surveyor), and they drew up a plan, with maps, for the drainage of the whole area. This entails digging a ditch with a number of tributaries from close to the back of the camp (north side) right over to the 'other' river, into a backwater of which the ditch will spill; and also a ditch of some length on the bank of our river, below the camp.

I have done my best to impress on Nobusawa and Sergeant Eda, his Number Two, the importance of this work if a great deal of malaria is not to occur. Duncan Black, who has established a curious ascendancy over Nobusawa, has really done the bulk of the work, but I have managed to interest Eda. We have had very great difficulty in impressing our own people with the urgency of organising strong parties of diggers. They are under great pressure from the Japs to supply the maximum numbers for work on the railway, but they are not quick to appreciate the importance of anti-malarial precautions and produce very few workers. In addition, there are very great difficulties in getting spades, chunkuls, picks and other tools. McCutcheon makes unsparing efforts, but the results are rather meagre.

Our command, especially Colonel Williamson, seemed most reluctant to approach the Japanese (though Duncan and I had already primed Nobusawa and Co.) but ultimately did so, and secured authority to draw a number of spades. Today we got eight spades and ten shovels – our best bag yet – and work has begun on the area close to the camp. This should not take very long, although the only labour I have been given are officers, who are very unskilled as compared with the agricultural workers of the Eastern Counties regiments we have with us. But these, HQ tells me, can't be spared from the railway. The officers too are rather unwilling to do this work – apart from a few.

25 November 1942

The small area on our bank has been completed – breeding areas are clear of water and the drain that carried it off is being oiled. We get some anti-malarial (old engine) oil from the Japanese now. Work has now begun on the huge area behind the camp extending across to the other river. This is a large undertaking, and a lot of water is involved. McCutcheon and Perkins have marked out the line of their main drain. There is a fairly good-sized party of officers detailed for this scheme. Some of them are hard workers but a number are very reluctant and Major W——— heads a party that holds that this work should not be done by officers. If it is not, of course, it won't be done at all. I did my best to persuade him that it was vital for the camp, but I believe he has refused to cooperate and may be 'court-martialled'. The party is got together each morning and HQ should of course arrange for the whole job to be done by their own executives. But nine times out of ten I am asked to speak to the Japanese about tools, in obtaining which there is great difficulty. I do not think HQ really try – they don't like talking to the Japs any more than I do – but this work is really urgent.

The other day Skinner (HQ) solemnly told me that it would be inadvisable to ask the Japs for any tools that day as Lieutenant Gota was annoyed about the disappearance of a spade (not used by the anti-malarial gang at all). I at once went to see Nobusawa and Sergeant Eda; the latter came with me to Lieutenant Gota's office and without any difficulty was authorised to draw 20 spades from the Jap store. I think the Korean, Matsuoka, who looks after the store, is the chief source of trouble. For a day or two we got on quite well but, Gota having left the camp, Matsuoka is cutting down the number of the tools he issues and what I do get tend to be damaged or weak. If I protest to Matsuoka, he just shouts abuse at me and I make no progress. Sergeant Eda helps when he can, but being in the medical office he has no real authority over Matsuoka who in Gota's absence is supreme – and he is entirely indifferent to anti-malarial work, as well as on bad terms with the medical side. Though, as I say, some of the officers on the digging party are hard working and keen, some are very much not so. They are very careless with the tools (I can't say I altogether blame them) and have broken one or two, which has caused furious outbursts from Matsuoka.

A pleasant surprise today: Ian came up from Ban Pong. Conditions are still squalid and wet down there. Davies is better – he has diphtheria.

The new hospital building is advancing very slowly – the work is being done by officers under Marsh's direction. The officers have to bring the big bamboo poles and the attap to the hospital area from the river bank 300 yards away. They find when they have carried it up ready to begin work that Japanese or Korean soldiers, who are supervising hut building not far away, bring *their* parties over to the officers' dump and take the material away for their huts. They protest in vain. So progress is slow. Marsh is putting in a lot of work, and Balfour is doing his best to get latrines prepared near the site of the new buildings to obviate unnecessary delay in their occupation.

The Japanese, our HQ think, are toying with the idea of making all officers work. The hospital hut-building and the anti-malarial drain-digging, which we have arranged ourselves in our own interests, may be regarded as the thin end of the wedge: though in principle working on the railway purely for the Japs is a different matter.

Under the portion of the Geneva Convention which I believe the Japanese have signed, officer prisoners cannot be compelled to work though other ranks may.[1] But while I think it reasonable that our HQ should decide to order officers to do the anti-malarial and the hospital building work, I do not think they would be justified in agreeing to officers working on the railway. Actually Colonel Williamson told Duncan Black and myself that 'in return for certain concessions' from the Japs the battalion COs had unanimously agreed that officers should do certain work about the camp for our own health. The 'certain concessions' are presumably the abandonment of the supposed Japanese threat to employ officers on railway work. It is far from clear that they have as yet actually threatened to do this. There is a widespread feeling that our HQ are too compliant with Japanese demands. There is also a good deal of doubt whether in fact Colonel Williamson has received *any* explicit 'concessions' from the Japanese.[2]

26 November 1942

Last night about 4am the siren in the paper factory at Kanburi began to wail and shortly after several multi-engined planes went over, going west. It was a sinister but thrilling sound; none of us felt much doubt these were Allied planes. This morning the Japanese say they were Chinese. We feel much cheered up. These machines may have been returning from bombing in the Bangkok area. The local Thais seem rather pleased: they dislike the Japs. The weather now is extremely good. There has been no rain for a considerable time and it is very cool at night – last night actually chilly. During the day there is a pleasantly cool north-easterly breeze. One never wears a shirt during

---

[1] Article 49 of the 1929 Geneva Convention stated that officers 'may in no circumstances be compelled to work'. Japan signed the Convention but never ratified it. After the outbreak of war the Japanese government gave an assurance that though not legally bound by the Geneva Convention it would in general respect its terms. In practice, it flagrantly and cynically contravened them.

[2] Note by RSH. Looking back and having in mind the deceit and evasiveness of the Japs, one can't but think one was rather hard on our camp administration. But there was too much secretiveness and equivocation within our own side.

the day, and many people are extraordinarily brown. Cooking has improved with the elaboration of the cooking accommodation by all sorts of improvisations; altogether with eggs, bananas and peanut toffee our diet is not at all bad and I for one am thriving on it. The trouble is the shortage, or rather absence, of special foodstuffs for people who are sick.

The railway cutting through the limestone shoulder near the camp is progressing very slowly. An engineer tells me the Japanese don't seem to know much about the job, but they are making progress.

9 December 1942

Yesterday was the anniversary of the outbreak of the war in the Far East. It passed uncelebrated. Since I wrote last, the new hospital buildings have been completed and occupied, and Major Pemberton RAMC (a New Zealand surgeon and an energetic and conscientious person) is in command. The hospital medical officers are Hendry, Welsh, Gotla, Meldrum, Ian and myself. De Wardener[1] will join as soon as Walker comes up from Ban Pong to take over No. 3 Battalion from him.

The difficulty of procuring medical supplies from the Japanese continues. We have nearly 350 cases of active malaria and quinine is doled out to us in small quantities without any system. The malarias are still in the hut ends in the main camp, the new hospital and the isolation building being occupied by skins, dysenteries, diphtherias and some vitamin deficiencies. Diphtheria and dysentery are the two dangerous conditions at present, and deaths are occurring. The sort of thing that happens is exemplified by Elvidge. He began with acute dysentery; in the middle of it he got malaria, and before that had settled developed diphtheria (faucial) and had to have a tracheotomy. He had no blanket and one of the officers of his battalion, who had three, refused to lend him one. He would have died anyway, but this incident gave rise to comment.

Work on the great anti-malaria scheme continues. It has been speeded up of late by the intervention of Lieutenant Matsumoto, who arrived the other day from up-river with the anti-malarial party under Cecil Lea. This party has been up-river at least two months: they got very bad food up there and were in poor shape with malaria, ulcers and sores, and Vitamin B deficiencies. Sandie Massie was specially bad. Matsumoto, who had learned something about anti-malarial work from Lea, who is a planter, 'approved' of my anti-malarial scheme and supported it and today we were actually given a large party of other ranks as well as the usual officer party, and an adequate number of tools. There were nearly 150 men working out there. It looked an impressive sight. The work went on very quickly; the outfall should be completed at this rate in a day or two, and a huge area of water will be drained off. McCutcheon has done what he could to oil these great areas with 'anti-malarial' oil supplied by the Japanese, but his efforts have probably not been very effective since with so much impenetrable bamboo, islands in deep water and so on, not all the dangerous areas can be reached. In any case it was not till a few days ago that we had enough oil to tackle these.

[1] Hugh de Wardener, later Professor of Medicine, University of London, Charing Cross Hospital.

Matsumoto, a cadet officer, is said to be the only officer concerned with field work on malaria in this area. Lea says that when he took over the anti-malarial party he knew nothing at all about mosquitoes. The work they did up-country at Lea's suggestion was quite sensible, but would have no permanent effect, though Matsumoto appeared to believe that wherever they had been they had abolished malaria for all time.

A Japanese medical unit at Kanburi, under a Captain Sakai, has given proof of its incompetence in another direction. They came up here to take blood films from all the malaria cases in camp, and insisted on taking these films from men who had been under treatment for some days with quinine. Even so they reported 29 positive out of 110 – a quite reasonable result really with the five-day course in force at present. The positives would in general be the men in their first day, since quinine very quickly clears the peripheral blood of parasites even in the reduced doses which we have to give. I think the malarial peak is still to come in spite of our draining and oiling. The work has been far too slowly carried out.

14 December 1942

The hospital continues to increase in size as new buildings are added. There are now two complete huts, and the central building (office and operating room) is now under construction. Two more 50-metre huts are projected. A large number of diphtheria cases have come down from Wang Lan camp 9–10 kilometres away: some are very severe. There have already been several deaths from diphtheria, and dysentery also takes its toll, do what we will. I look after the bulk of the malarias in hospital and have been lucky in having no cerebral or blackwater case so far. I have not had much time for anti-malarial work outside the camp. The drainage into the 'other' river has not been carried through yet. The big parties which Matsumoto secured dwindled rapidly after he went (which was after a day or two). I am not convinced that our HQ made any effort to maintain the numbers of the party, though from our point of view the work was much more important than the work on the railway. I know it is difficult for them to press the Japs, but I feel they have given up trying. With 350–400 cases under treatment (between 50 and 100 new cases per day) they don't seem to take the malaria question seriously.

Supplies of quinine are inadequate and my daily supplications to Nobusawa continue.

I hope the malarial drain will be completed in a day or two. It still has 47 officers and 12 other ranks working on it, and working quite well.

21 December 1942

There has been a lot of anxiety and difficulty over diphtheria cases. We have of course constantly been pressing the Japanese for antitoxin – Duncan Black and Max Pemberton have had endless interviews with Nobusawa. At first he did not question that they were diphtheria cases; but he said that he had no antitoxin and that as Thailand was so backward he could not get any. This is obviously nonsense – there is a famous Pasteur Institute in Bangkok not far away. But Nobusawa was clearly not going to bother himself about it. Several officers and men died of diphtheria during this period, and finally after continuous pressure Nobusawa asked us to take throat swabs of all cases, saying that if they were positive he would try to get some antitoxin. The swabs were taken to him in a couple of hours. For six days now we have been asking him for the results, but can get no information – the swabs are supposed to have been sent to a Japanese field laboratory at Kanburi. Meantime he has actually given us 12,500 units of antitoxin – enough for perhaps one case under civilised conditions. Nobusawa says the Japanese will themselves take swabs in future. The number of fresh cases is now fortunately diminishing. For two whole days Nobusawa refused to do anything but fish in the river; we had to go down to the bank to make representations. Squatting there with his fishing rod, he would wave us away, saying, 'Holiday, holiday.' He made no attempt to do anything at all, even to be civil.

Another crisis which caused some excitement was over the question of officers working on the railway line. The Japanese finally said they must work and that they would use extreme measures to obtain compliance with this order. (Colonel Yanagida, the Jap camp commandant, had discreetly left the camp a few days earlier leaving Osato, presumably with his instructions, in charge.) They paraded the officers in the morning and called out an armed Jap party, who lined up, loaded their rifles and stood ready. Our senior officers decided to comply, and I think the great majority of the officers concerned were in agreement with this decision. It did not really seem worthwhile to commit suicide over this question. The two engineer officers, Kiriama and Tarimoto, were the moving spirits in these proceedings. Osato, a spineless creature, was pushed on by them. Nobusawa was supposed to weed out the officers who were not fit; but at the parade at which he was to do this, the engineer officers turned up and in the most blatant manner insisted on his passing men that they considered looked well enough, while he sheepishly stood by. He made no pretence of examining cases with special histories (for example, an officer with a long history of stone in the kidney) but simply waved them away to the working group.

As a result of this the anti-malarial party and the hospital building party have been reduced, but not, I am glad to say, abolished altogether.

There has been brutal manhandling of Thais by the Jap guards – they say they have been caught buying clothing from prisoners. The guards have also become more offensive and violent towards us.

All sick men who are not working, and all hospital patients, now have to wear a red tape round their arm. The Japanese evidently think that a lot of men who are fit are dodging work.

Today we were given printed postcards to send off – no writing except a name in a space provided ('Please see that . . . is taken care') and a signature. This is the second card we have sent off since capture. The first was in June, just before we left Singapore.

The malaria wards continue busy – anything from 15 to 20 admissions to hospital per day. Many cases of malaria are of course not sent into hospital at all.

25 December 1942

Today is a whole holiday by courtesy of the Japanese. Special meals are being cooked in the cookhouses, and Hajji Marsh, Ian, Duncan and myself are cooking a special meal in Ian's lean-to – omelettes, pancakes and some chicken. There was some carol singing last night and this morning. One can't but feel a certain melancholy at spending Christmas in this depressing camp. An almost intolerable sense of oppression and futility overcomes one at times, as month after wasted month passes. At this time, of course, one thinks much of home, and one realises they must be going through a period of anxiety. And there are many at home who have yet to learn that their relatives out here are already dead. Henry Mills, whom Ian and I knew well and who was wounded badly in Perak and marked for evacuation from Malaya (but wasn't, because of the incompetence of the medical arrangements in Singapore) has died up-river, we have heard. And there are 20 graves already in this camp alone.

Read has come up from Ban Pong and becomes OC Hospital, Pemberton becoming surgical specialist. I think he made a very good hospital commandant. Read is as conscientious, but he is more disillusioned and as a result, I think, gets rather less response out of the Japs, who are quick to detect, and resent, anything in the nature of irony.

Colonel Williamson has been making trouble with the anti-malarial party. He told Captain Andrews yesterday that I was very dissatisfied with the officers in the party. It is true that I was very dissatisfied at the beginning, but I have more than once recently told Colonel Williamson that they were doing very much better, and I actually said so in writing in a report which I submitted to him a few days ago urging the necessity of keeping a sufficient number of men on this work. But apparently the Japs are trying to get more officers out working on the railway and it looks as if Colonel Williamson, anxious as ever to comply, was trying to put the blame on me for the necessity of turning the anti-malarial party officers on to railway work. The time is approaching when upkeep of the anti-malarial drains will be the main part of the work, and there is no question that a party of officers (some of them at least must be planters who know what they are about in anti-malarial work) will do upkeep work much better than other ranks. So I shall strain every nerve to maintain a party of officers for this work. The number of fresh malaria cases is on the whole tending to fall, though relapses are no less numerous: but there is no ground for optimism or relaxation of effort.

Occasional cases of diphtheria are still occurring. The Japanese lab has reported all the swabs, both ours and the ones they have taken themselves, negative, and hence Nobusawa says that there are no cases of diphtheria in this camp: so he will provide no further antitoxin. Similarly these Japanese pathologists have reported that all the specimens from dysentery patients which they have examined have not shown any dysentery organisms, hence they take the view that there is no dysentery in this camp. And yet many prisoners perversely continue to die.

28 December 1942

The night before last, about 3am, the sound of multi-engined planes was heard again. It was a bright moonlit night, but we could not see anything in the sky. The Kanburi siren went and the traffic overhead continued for about an hour. Towards the end, the detonations of bombs were very faintly audible in the extreme distance.

Yesterday McCutcheon, Smith Laing, Longbottom and I climbed the big hill near here and saw, faint on the eastern horizon, three smoke columns rising into the air in the direction of Bangkok.

There are all sorts of rumours – of landings at Akyab and Mergui – but they are probably the result of excitement from hearing the planes. I tackled Colonel Williamson about his remark to Captain Andrews of the anti-malarial party. He said there was a misunderstanding and that he would speak to Captain Andrews. Captain Andrews's continued remoteness when I speak to him does not lead me to think that Colonel Williamson has admitted to misrepresenting my views. I am told that the maintenance party is to be other ranks after all.

7 January 1943

Another year is beginning. The Japanese anti-malarial party (Cecil Lea's lot) has gone away up-river again: but they have left behind a fair amount of oil for maintenance here. And McCutcheon has remained with six officers (not men) to carry on the work. We have found anophelines recently breeding in the padi on the other side of the railway.

Hospital conditions continue difficult, with great overcrowding and utterly inadequate dressings. Quinine has been adequate recently but the pressure of numbers makes it necessary to turn men out before they are fit again.

Permission has been obtained for lights to be burned up to 10pm in the officers' part of the 'canteen' at night. There are tables and benches there. One supplies one's own light – a half tin with a wick supported in oil – and Bill Adams, Basil Peacock, Tom Watson and I have a regular four there from 8 to 10pm. But this does not seem likely to go on for long as there are rumours of the camp being broken up and fit men sent up-river to new camps.

Abron (sub-tertian malaria) threw a violent fit in the malaria ward at about midnight. He made a terrific noise. I had to give him half a grain of morphia. It is difficult coping with cases like this in a dark hut, crammed with men, by the light of an oil flare.

14 January 1943

Another quarrel with HQ. McCutcheon told me today that he is under orders to go up-country with a detachment under Colonel Johnson. He is my chief anti-malarial officer and very important for the health of this camp, but I was not consulted. I was going to make a strong protest but it became clear that most of McCutcheon's friends were going in that party and that I would probably be going with another myself. So I decided to give up the struggle. The actual digging is all finished. All that is necessary now is upkeep and oiling. I shall hand over supervision to Ian, who will be staying on here when I go, and he will fix up a party (there are other Malayan planters available) and they can be shown around by McCutcheon and Co. before he leaves.

Yesterday, with Duncan Black, David Arkush and the Jap interpreter, Fulda, I paid a visit to Kanburi to get some supplies in view of my forthcoming move up-river. I bought a zinc pail, a kettle, a blanket (very poor quality), some soap and toothpaste. We had a pleasant meal (rice and tomato omelette) at a new eating place by the town gate.

It has been very cold at night recently and my new blanket plus my old thin one were nothing like enough last night. I wore pyjamas, khaki drill trousers, sleeveless jumper, windjacket and socks and only just didn't freeze. How the troops who in the hot weather recklessly sold their shirts, pants and blankets manage, I can't imagine. A good many of them get up and walk about, and others congregate in the cookhouses.

The up-river move has begun. The 4th Battalion (mostly 5th Suffolks) went four days ago, and others are to follow in the next week or two.

The moon is waxing again and is very brilliant at night. The constellations are very clear and bright after dark – Perseus and Andromeda and Auriga with Capella; Hyades and Pleiads, Orion and Sirius, and Canopus, Achernar and Fomalhaut low down in a line above the southern horizon. In the early morning before dawn, the moon having set, the sky is brilliant with A and B Centauri and the Southern Cross in the south; overhead, Boötes, the Northern Crown, the Lion and the Crab with Denebola; Regulus and Arcturus blazing like planets; and the Plough.

Padi near Kanburi camp

15 January 1943

Besides being charged 45 ticals per month for food and shelter (I spoke of this before) we have for the last two months been charged 15 ticals per month for clothing, which is deducted from our supposed monthly pay. All the clothes I've had have been one pair of canvas shoes so small that I can't wear them. Someone has calculated that the total sum which the officers are taxed would cover the total cost of supplying the camp, men as well as officers.

Food is tending to go up in price, and it is not so easy as it was to obtain eggs, onions, sugar and biscuits.

One would not mind paying 15 ticals a month if we got anything for it. Many people have no towels, their only shorts are filthy and in ribbons, they have no shirts, no boots. Soap is expensive and men who are not getting enough to eat in their rations are reluctant to spend money on anything but the vital extra food.

Very occasionally there is a general issue of soap but it is so small – each man receives no more than will last three to four days at most – and so rarely (once in five or six weeks) that it makes no real difference.

Recently officers' contributions to men's messing have been about 5 ticals each per month, with 2 to 3 ticals for the hospital. As there are about 200 officers in the camp the sums produced are quite substantial and have made a great difference to the men's food, and have been the means of providing a lot of eggs and milk for patients in hospital. Now a new scheme is proposed by which, out of the balances which are, we are told, banked for us, we shall contribute about 10 ticals a month, so as to give the hospital a monthly income of about 2,000 ticals. As the Japanese evidently will not supply the hospital with any special foods, and only a token issue of drugs, we have to try to buy such things ourselves.

21 January 1943

Yesterday we received our January pay – 30 ticals – and signed for 40, the extra 10 ticals being transferred direct to the hospital. One would like to know whether this is the maximum amount that the Japanese will allow to be transferred, and whether in fact the sum thus arrived at will be as much as will be required. One hopes that camps where there are only a few officers will be able to benefit by having money sent to them. At all events the scheme represents an advance in the attempt to cope with dietary deficiencies and illness.

I know now that I am to go to Wan Tow Kien at the end of this month, with Duncan Black. Robson, who has been there for a bit, says there is some malaria there. McCutcheon and Smith Laing are going up to Bankao, about 8 kilometres further on. Moir, who came down from there two days ago, says Wan Tow Kien is fairly good as regards accommodation and that the Japanese commandant is not severe. But food, he says, is rather poor, and supplementary items expensive and hard to get.

23 January 1943

As a result of the 10 ticals for the hospital being paid out of our 'savings bank balances', not out of the 30 we are actually paid, our contribution to the men's messing has been stepped up. This is all to the good; but the financing of men not working (and therefore not being paid) but not in hospital has not been faced up to. Some units have funds with which they enable these men to buy extras. But some have not; and men are constantly being left behind in camps when their own units go on elsewhere. There are then no funds to help such people.

Sick men are coming down to us here from camps up-river, particularly Wang Lan, 9 or 10 kilometres away. Another base hospital was going to open at Kanburi about now, we were told, but nothing has happened about this yet. We were to have sent cases there from our hospital here. We now have 550 men in hospital here. The diet has been improved and practically everyone in hospital gets at least one duck's egg a day. We can now buy meat for general messing for the men: a beast costs 12–15 ticals – very good value. And the canteens sell extra food and fruit. But the 'Attend Cs', who don't draw pay as they can't work, need more help.

Wan Tow Kien

Wan Tow Kien

4 February 1943

I have now been in Wan Tow Kien for four days. I came up by barge (towed by a launch) to Wang Lan – a slow but quite pleasant journey. I spent the night at Wang Lan, getting a very good dinner from Boswell, the quartermaster, in company with Tommy Broughton and Bill Goddard. I slept on my bedding roll on the floor of a hut close to the river, carefully spreading my mosquito net. During the night I heard the splashing of big fish in the river close by. Next morning, I went by lorry (carrying rations) over open padi land and through thick bamboo jungle for what seemed miles and miles, bumped violently up and down as I sprawled on top of a heap of miscellaneous vegetables. At one time when I flattened myself out to avoid overhanging branches which continuously whipped over the open lorry my elbow became deeply embedded in a large squashy pumpkin. I found the journey more exhausting than pleasant.

Arrived at Wan Tow Kien I joined the 5th Suffolks officers' mess. They are an extremely pleasant crowd. The hospital is small and is not loaded over its capacity. Duncan Black arrived two days after me with money for the hospital, some blankets and some mosquito nets. Perkins, Peter Shearlaw and David Stewart have also come here, as an anti-malarial party. Andrews and Tommy Ross have gone on to Bankao to join McCutcheon. The weather is gradually getting warmer, but is very fine.

15 February 1943

Today is the grievous anniversary of the fall of Singapore. We hope we do not have to spend another under like conditions. Things are not going too badly here. The hospital is full, but not unduly so; there is no gross lack for once of drugs or materials. The local Japanese or Korean medical corporal is quite reasonable and we get enough quinine for treatment. The hospital diet, liberally subsidised by the funds brought up by Duncan, is very good. Excellent Japanese strawberry jam at 55 cents a tin makes some very good sweets.

There is not much malaria in this camp, though there is a dengue-like low fever from which I am suffering myself at the moment. It is not severe. Bill Adams has joined the anti-malarial party at my instance and they are oiling the possible breeding places round the camp. My jungle walks, sometimes with the anti-malarial party on their rounds, sometimes with one or other of them just for the exercise and sense of freedom, are most enjoyable. There are some small orchids here and there on the trees. We see jungle fowl quite often, and there are attractive views along the river. We have also located an abandoned orchard of lime trees, in which there is quite a lot of ripe fruit.

Some Dutch troops from Java (Europeans and Eurasians) are passing through on their way up-river. There are said to be more to come. A lot of Japanese aeroplanes have been going over east–west and west–east.

21 February 1943

A good many Dutch have gone through. They have left behind a number of sick, mostly an obstinate type of dysentery, more severe often than the dysenteries we have seen so much of. Three battalions have just gone up-river from here to Bankao. The hospital is getting crowded. Big parties of sick are coming down from up-river suffering from severe beriberi, dysentery, diphtheria, huge ulcers, frightful scabies and all manner of weakness and prostration owing to overwork on poor diets. We pass all the bad cases down to Chungkai where they can cope with them better.

Apart from No. 1 Battalion, which goes up-river tomorrow, there are none but sick in the camp, and it is half-deserted and melancholy. Time drags wearily on. How long is this existence going to last? And how will it end, I wonder? In disaster for many?

There have been some heavy showers recently.

27 February 1943

The hospital goes fairly well: we have been able to get our 'chronics' off to Chungkai. The Korean medical corporal, Kanehara, has been unusually amiable. Read sent up a case of milk and some morphia recently. Conditions at Bankao, not far from here, are rather bad, we hear. There is not enough accommodation and many, including sick, are having to sleep in the open. The worst cases from time to time come down here, and if possible we send them on to Chungkai. Parties going up-country occasionally stop here for a night. The railway track in this section has been finished and the gang laying the metals is getting quite near.

Yesterday by arrangement I walked up the line towards Bankao and met and had a talk with McCutcheon, Brownie Smith Laing, Longbottom and Tommy Ross. There have been one or two more deaths here among the Dutch – a severe type of dysentery, and one diphtheria as well.

I am not particularly busy – the hospital is now quite small and easily manageable. I sit and read or darn my socks (an endless struggle), or occasionally do a crossword (the book of a hundred *Times* crosswords which Margaret gave me for the journey to Australia in 1941 is invaluable and has lasted amazingly), play patience, or just meditate, usually on the question of how long this existence is going to continue. Food here is fairly good: extras are available even if expensive. We have had some cocoa, and with eggs and sugar and some tins of strawberry jam we have managed to make some very delicious sweet omelettes on our frying plate over a bamboo fire.

1 March 1943

My birthday today, an occasion which I note with little enthusiasm. This is

Top: Page from Robert Hardie's sketchbook, 1943. Bottom: Wan Tow Kien camp, 10 February 1943

the second birthday I have spent in captivity and I hope it may be the last. The past twelve months have, I suppose, passed fairly quickly but they have been weary months, full of depression and boredom and vain hopes. One thing I have reason to be deeply thankful for is that I have kept well. I hope I manage to remain so.

3 March 1943

We have had another big batch of sick[1] down from Bankao, most of whom have already gone on to Chungkai. There were among them a fractured fore-arm and a case of keratitis with hypopion, both of whom had been waiting the Japs' pleasure to come down for three or four days. The man with the keratitis is likely to lose his eye as a result of the delay. It is extraordinary that after more than eight months in Thailand the arrangements for moving desperately ill men down to base camps are still so utterly chaotic and supplies and equipment so utterly inadequate. As time goes on the Japanese, instead of improving these things, seem to be becoming more completely indifferent.

[1] Note by RSH. One of them I remember, Millar a miner from Dalkeith, in the last stages of dysentery and beriberi. He was pretty helpless, but uncomplaining. We had no bedpans of course; the bad cases were put as near the latrines as possible and the orderlies helped. Miller had to struggle out in the middle of the night. As I was helping him back to his sleeping place he said, 'Oh my, Oh my,' and was dead.

No attempt is being made to provide shelter for the men, including sick, who have to sleep in the open at Bankao. It is the same in camps further up the river, one hears. The insistence on men, more men, to work on the railway construction goes hand in hand with a total absence of any effort to produce conditions in which they can keep fit. It is rumoured that our men are to be up here for the next seven or eight months, through the rainy season; if this is the case better shelter will have to be provided. The rails have already been laid past this camp.

Duncan Black has been having dysentery – checked by emetine injections, so presumably it is amoebic. We have of course no microscope for diagnosis.

Margaret's birthday yesterday. I hope she is all right. It is depressing having no news at all from home. I hope Mother, Frank and Colin[1] are all right too. I wonder always how soon I shall see them all again.

9 March 1943

Lice have appeared in these huts – I found one or two in my clothes yesterday, but by energetic action have got rid of them for the time being at least. Bugs have been with us constantly, but lice are rather more sinister, and perhaps have something to do with the eight to ten days' fever that a number of people are getting. It is mild – far from classical typhus in severity – and it has none of the accompaniments of Malayan scrub typhus.

There is also a rumour of cholera up-river. Cholera is of course endemic in this country. As there is no cholera vaccine, the Japs are issuing dysentery vaccine instead. They have some, a speciality of their own, of dubious value even against dysentery.

As a result of the prolonged dry season, a lot of the trees round here are more or less leafless at present, and their pale silvery branches against the deep blue skies are very lovely to look at. But one longs for the Scottish spring, with peewits tumbling and calling, and the early buds on birches and beeches – I am thinking of a fishing holiday at Monimusk on the Don in April 1924.

13 March 1943

No. 3 Battalion has come back to this camp from up-river. 180 of them and four officers were sent off at short notice to join the telegraph line party under Martens and Adams (both Volunteer officers). Most of the sick from Bankao have come down here, and some of them have been sent on to Chungkai today.

This camp is again crowded and the Korean guards from Bankao, whose behaviour up there was detestable, are now here. We had a taste of this when playing bridge last night at the end of the hut. The guard made a point of walking up and down past us and other groups at the ends of other huts and each time he passed we all had to get up and stand at attention. It is unspeakably humiliating to have to comply with the caprices of these coolies: but refusal, we know from people from Bankao, leads to savage beatings-up. Under the Japanese system, one has no protection or redress against this kind of thing.

[1] RSH's two brothers, later respectively President of Corpus Christi College, Oxford, and Honorary Professor of Ancient Literature, Royal Academy of Arts.

Boy at Wan Tow Kien, 10 March 1943

19 March 1943

A pleasant walk with Basil yesterday to the summit of a little rocky hill a couple of miles from this camp, giving a good view up the river valley to the higher hills in the distance. It has become clear that we are all going further up-river shortly, beyond the No. 4 Group camps, where we believe a lot of the Volunteers are. Black and I are to go, taking with us the hospital staff we have here, and getting, we hope, transport. All the unfit are to be sent down to Chungkai before we go. Bill Adams should go down with them perhaps, but he doesn't want to (the anti-malarial party is part of the hospital staff) and in the absence of data of any kind it is impossible to judge what is best. One simply doesn't know whether conditions where we are going will be better or worse than here or at Chungkai.

In the last month or two I have read a number of good books – mostly reread, to be precise. *Waverley*, Churchill's *The World Crisis, The Pickwick Papers, David Copperfield, The Return of the Native, Pride and Prejudice* and Bridges's *Testament of Beauty*. It is surprising how many people have books like these which they cling to through thick and thin.

23 March 1943

I have just got back to Wan Tow Kien after two days down at Chungkai. I went down accompanying a party of 110 sick, 60 of them Dutch from Tarkilin, a camp 15 kilometres or so above here. They were mostly beriberi, pellagra and dysentery, this last in some cases very severe, but as this camp has to be evacuated shortly we had to send them off as the Japanese would not hear of their staying here even for a day or two, although some of them are quite unfit to travel under prevailing conditions. Many of them were in a desperate state after their journey down by barge the day before.

We left in the early morning. The Japanese allowed one lorry to make one trip to the station, which is about three kilometres away from this camp, with ten sick men who couldn't walk. One man had to be carried the whole way on a stretcher. Others who could not walk had to be helped by parties of fit men who carried them on their backs or sitting on their clasped hands, in relays. It was an exhausting journey even over that short distance, along a very irregular narrow dirty track through the jungle. It was very hard work for the fit men but they did very well – even so it was absolutely prostrating for these fearfully sick men, some of them mere skeletons, gaunt, fleshless and despairing. It would have been so easy to have a train stopped on the line where it passes close to the camp: but even if the Japanese POW administration were prepared to consider doing such a thing (which they are not) it is certain that the railway staff, which is independent and quite regardless of the convenience of other branches of the Japanese army, let alone of the prisoners, would not attempt to fall in with the proposal.

It was a blazing hot day. When we got to the station, the Jap guards compelled us to load the helpless sick into open trucks standing in the sun, and there they lay for an hour before the train started. We had only our water bottles: we haven't the containers to carry extra water on trips like these. When we reached Wang Lan station we again stood in the sun for an hour. Some British other ranks working at the station were able to let the sick have a little drinkable water. Then on again to Chungkai, where the train stopped 400–500 yards from the nearest part of the camp. We lifted the sick out, and sent into the camp for help. This took some time in arriving and the Jap guards with us became very excited and insisted on the sick being made to walk in. Some of them simply could not attempt it; but fortunately the guards did not actually become violent and ultimately they were all got back to the camp.

River Kwai Noi near Wan Tow Kien camp

As the last one was starting back David Arkush and a friend of his, Charles Fisher[1], came out and helped me in with my bedroll and haversack. David found me a place in his hut, and as soon as I arrived gave me a huge cup of coffee – I was so dehydrated that my Eustachian tubes must have collapsed or got gummed up, and I was extremely deaf. But after a lot of fluid I felt better. Going without water a whole day in the sun, without any preparation, makes one realise what thirst is.

It was pleasant to see Ian and other friends at Chungkai. I learned that Max Pemberton and a party of six medical officers and 60 orderlies were coming up to the new up-river camp where Duncan Black and I are going. They have had news in Chungkai that Graham Taylor of the Chartered Bank, Singapore, has died of dysentery up at a Group 4 camp. There is a rumour, too, that Cecil Lea has died up-country of diphtheria.[2]

[1] Later Professor of Geography, School of Oriental and African Studies, University of London.
[2] Note by RSH. Subsequently found not to be true.

Chungkai was much improved since I left. There is a good canteen service and food of all kinds is obtainable – coffee, lime juice, cakes, eggs, peanuts, bananas and so on at reasonable prices. I felt it would be quite a good place to be staying in.

We do not know quite what our work will be when we get up to our camp, which the Japanese say is close to Burma. It may be railway or road-making.

My journey back to Wan Tow Kien was quicker and much easier, as I travelled alone with a Korean guard. To catch the train, we had to walk right down to the river junction at Kanburi, cross and go through the town to the train-stopping place half a mile on the far side, beyond the 'Aerodrome' camp. Fortunately, or rather with this in view, I had little kit with me, though my haversack was considerably weighed down by six tins of strawberry jam which I had bought in Chungkai. We started at a little before dawn from Chungkai, the full moon setting behind us over the hills to the north-west. The walk was cool and pleasant along the riverside path – we were walking almost due east – and the sunrise that developed in front of us as the sun rose behind a ridge of low tree-fringed hills beyond Kanburi was extremely magnificent. At the confluence of the rivers we found a native canoe to take us over the 'other' river and so into Kanburi town and on to the railway. The train of three or four open light goods trucks was hauled by a heavy diesel truck fitted with steel-rimmed wheels to fit the railway. We rattled up to the wooden bridge across the 'other' river, crossed – in so doing we got a good view of the handsome concrete piers of the steel-spanned bridge they are building there – and ran over the flat towards the cutting close to Chungkai camp, through it and out on to the flat bamboo jungle which extends all the way up to Wan Tow Kien. There is something rather impressive about this rapidly-built narrow traffic line cut through the wilderness.

Now I am back in Wan Tow Kien waiting for the move up-river. The news we get is of activity in Tunis, and the Germans counter-attacking in the Donetz region to hold up the Russian advance.

March Up-River

March Up-River

8 April 1943

More than a fortnight since my last entry. On 28 March we were told that on the next day all fit men in the camp would be going on up-river, and all men not fit to do so must be ready to be evacuated down to Chungkai about the same time. Hiruda, a Korean corporal in charge of all the camp administration, assured Duncan Black that transport would be provided for all the hospital 'equipment' and staff, for the whole journey up-river. Next morning there was no transport to the station and we only managed to get our heavy stuff along with a great deal of labour. The troops going with us (about a thousand, I think) had all their cooking utensils to carry, but finally we all got along to the railway halt – a place where the jungle is cut back a little further than usual from the railway line and a short stretch of doubled line enables trains to pass. We dumped our heavy baggage beside the track and then settled down to wait, trying to find shade from the blazing sun – a difficult matter, as there was little else than bamboo and it was practically

Hills above 110 km camp

leafless. We sat waiting for some hours. The Jap guards, who were also annoyed by the delay and made enquiries at the halt office where there is a telephone, reported that the railway people knew nothing of any arrangements to take us up-country – no trains had been ordered to pick up a party of prisoners here.

Finally, however, well into the afternoon, a train came up and took half of us, and the whole of the hospital company, and off we rattled up the track. At the Bankao halt, which we reached very soon, more British troops were waiting to go up – they had been there since 8am. Then on to Nom Pradai, and on from there to Tarkilin, where we stopped for a bit. At this halt there were a hundred sick men waiting in what shade they could find near the track to go down to Chungkai. Some of them were very ill; two, in fact, were dead, and two more dying. The Japanese had insisted on all the sick being brought from the camp some distance away to wait for a train – which never came. This sick party had no spades to dig graves, even if they had had the strength to do so; the Japs had told them to leave the bodies behind, as it would not be permitted to take them on the train. We were kept in our train; and then about 5pm off we went again through the monotonous bamboo jungle, on to the end of the laid rails, at Aruhiru (called Arrowhill). The train could go no further so we were decanted there. Our baggage was stacked alongside the line and we waited for a bit. Then we were told that we had to march on about 5 kilometres to Wampo Central with what baggage we could carry. One or two men were left behind as a nominal guard for the baggage, which was stacked irregularly along about 150 yards of line: Sergeant Shearman, on account of his age, was detached from the hospital party for this purpose. The Japs said this baggage would be brought up by barge next day. Needless to say it was not.

At Aruhiru we had a few words with 'Lagi' Lang, who had recently arrived with 300 men (recovered sick) from Chungkai. The railway track beyond Aruhiru had not been finished and the walk which we had to do was along a very steep and irregular rocky slope high above the river. At one point a ledge was being blasted for the railway across the face of a precipice falling into an elbow of the river. In places the railway track was being shored up with concrete and big baulks of timber. We had a difficult scramble across this stretch, clutching what baggage we were carrying. On the far side we found that the track – a low earth embankment – was finished and it made easier walking, particularly as it was now dark. Finally, about 9pm, we branched off down a narrow path and found ourselves in Wampo Central camp. I felt fairly brisk myself, but Bill Adams and Duncan, who still has dysentery, were pretty weary. I had had to leave my bedding roll behind at the railhead, as it was too heavy to carry. The dubious assurance that we should have transport misled me into not making up a portable bundle of essentials.

We got accommodation for the night in a rough bamboo hut occupied chiefly by the Burmese elephant syces. It was a pleasure to meet here Clive Corke, Frank Walker, Romney, Edgar, Blomfield, S. J. Clark (terribly thin, in hospital under Pavillard's care with amoebic dysentery), K. G. Sinclair, Robertson (3 Volunteer Field Ambulance), Tilley, Thomson, de Marco, Pat Stewart, Voin and others. The officers in this camp have a separate hut and

Opposite, top: River craft, 10 April 1943. Bottom: Fishing, 10 April 1943

16/4/43

Top: 110 km camp, 14 April 1943. Bottom: River at 110 km camp, 15 April 1943

mess, and at the end of the hut they have big bamboo seats round a huge fire. Bill Adams and I enjoyed a couple of fried eggs and a large cup of coffee here, through the hospitality of Clive Corke. This camp seems to be well run: the OC is Colonel Lilly, who seems to be given a fairly free hand by the Jap officer in charge, Lieutenant Hatori; the camp is well situated on a stretch of level ground high above a shingly stretch of river.

Next morning we went on along the railway track to Wampo North where we found the camp of the 'communications party' (telegraph line party) under Adams, Martens, Hugh Munro, Gibson and others, and there we were put into barges to go about 600 yards up-river to avoid a sheer cliff face overhanging the river. Across this face a ledge for the railway line is being cut, but it was not far enough on for it to be possible for us to walk that way. Landing again on the far side of this cliff, we marched a little more than a kilometre through a neglected banana plantation and then some thick jungle, and finally came to a huddled group of low and ruinous huts right on the bank of the river, where a party of 300 British troops lived and had their being. They were under O'Neal, a captain in the Gurkhas.

We were given tents to sleep in (very crowded) and have settled down, having been here nearly a fortnight. Food has been only fair. Mr Pong[1] has been here with his barge. We buy some eggs, but not as many as we could do with. The bulk of our baggage has arrived here – I went down to Wampo North four days ago and found Sergeant Shearman there. I have lost one or two things – pinched by Japanese or Siamese – but nothing vital; and my bedding roll is intact.

21 April 1943

Still in 110 kilometre camp, in our crowded tent among the trees on the river bank. The railway lines have been laid as far as Wampo North, which means that the concrete-and-timber-supported track which we scrambled along just on this side of Aruhiru has been made passable. The precipice on this side of Wampo North is still the scene of heavy work, blasting and shovelling; but even here the ledge for the metals is said to be not far off completion.

I have caught a few river carp with a line and hooks which I have had with me since Singapore, using ripe pumpkin as bait. These carp, boiled in salt water, are extremely good to eat. The weather is becoming rather more showery and the river is rising a little and getting more turbid. The rainy season (South West Monsoon) has not begun yet, but it can't be far away. I have had one or two walks along the railway track to the north of here. There is a fine view up-river about a mile beyond the camp on the north side from close to the railway.

We often see monkeys (Krah) playing in the bushes on the other side of the river. In early mornings the gibbons can be heard hooting and whistling in the hills around. They make a terrific hullabaloo – a wild, abandoned but rather agreeable sound. There are birds of all sorts – kingfishers, bee-eaters, what look like spur-winged plovers, sandpipers, kites, ospreys or fish eagles,

[1] Note by RSH. An English-speaking Siamese merchant from Kanburi whose activities on the river – selling extra foodstuffs, bringing up torch batteries to work the secret wireless receiver and so forth – were of absolutely incalculable value to the prison camps up and down the river.

drongos, bulbuls (yellow-vented and crested), 'Straits robins', shamas and so forth. There is a lot of barge traffic on the river, towed by the little diesel-engined, single-cylinder boats, onomatopoeically called 'pom-poms'. Last night – the moon was nearly full but it was cloudy and rainy – we heard two big multi-engined planes go over.

27 April 1943

On 24 April we left 110 kilometre camp and marched up by the railway track and later by muddy lorry track to Tarsao, where we are now. The walk was not very interesting, apart from the fine views up-river from a point on the railway quite near 110 kilometre camp. Tarsao is a big camp, with a large area occupied by Japanese troops as well as a POW area. Colonel Harvey, RAMC, is OC Hospital. The food is pretty poor – but then we are only passing through and nobody here has much use for us. There is a fine view down the river from the bank near the POW cookhouses. A biggish bungalow is being built in the Japanese camp for, it is said, a Japanese general. The POWs who are building it take all the live bugs and lice they can find in their huts (and they find plenty), put them in matchboxes and let them out in the bungalow.

We are due to continue our march up-river tomorrow. Several battalions of 400 or so each will be going – they are all ready here now, having come up like us in the last few days.

5 May 1943

Early on the morning of 28 April we began our march up-river. The column consisted of about 650 men – a detachment of 400 other ranks and a group of about 250 officers. In addition there was my small hospital group – half a dozen other ranks and three 'anti-malarial' officers. Most carried all their worldly goods with them, but some, among them myself, left some additional articles with the 'heavy baggage' at Tarsao, to be brought up, we hoped, by barge or lorry later. We left behind in Tarsao also a number of men who had become sick since their arrival there, and were not fit for the march. Duncan Black stayed behind, as his dysentery had flared up again; and Bill Adams was prevailed on not to try the march, anxious as he was to come with us. He is over 50 and has had some enteritis; and doesn't look at all well. But I was sorry to part with him.

After lining up with all our burdens, and having been counted and recounted by anxious and impatient Japanese, we started off along the rough dust-and-mud track. It ran at first over the level river flats, through bamboo and small teak jungle, giving some grateful shade from the early sun. After half a dozen kilometres, the track began to rise, climbing into some rough hill country. The trees were bigger here, some enormous with smooth soaring branchless trunks rising to a high leafy head. As the track rose, we got some fine views back over the level ground on which Tarsao lies, in a wide amphitheatre of jagged limestone hills, irregularly bisected by the river. The blue cloud sha-

Opposite, top: View up-river from 110 km camp. Bottom: View downstream from Tarsao

View downstream from Tarsao, 29 April 1943

dows, moving over the great expanses of varied greens, made an attractive picture.

Near the top of the climb we crossed the railway trace, which ran from right to left, swinging in towards the river after having made a wide detour from Tarsao to the east to gain height. We saw some members of the telegraph line party working here, putting up poles. The ground flattened out a bit now though it was still very rough and irregular. Not long after midday we came to a primitive camp beside a big spring among some high trees; there were one or two bamboo huts and some tents. All round were the forest trees and a dense undergrowth of broken branches, tree trunks and bamboo. Here we were to stay the night; and as it was still quite early in the day, we had time to wash in the stream after it had left the pools of the springs. There was a good deal to do, attending to blistered feet and seeing people who were feeling ill. The cooks managed to produce a meal of rice and vegetable stew; most people had a few hard-boiled eggs, laid in at Tarsao in anticipation of the journey. We slept crammed in our tents on the damp ground. At Colonel Johnson's request I took over medical supervision of the officers' battalion and the more thankless job of arguing with the Japanese in charge of our party about the disposal of sick men who were unable to keep on with the march. The track on which we were travelling was just adequate for vehicles so that if we did have to leave men behind they could be brought on by lorry. At this camp we did not have to ask for any such assistance however.

Camp in clearing near Kanyu, 29 April 1943

Next morning we started again shortly after dawn, thus making use of the cool part of the day. It was a short march again, ending about midday, this time in a wide natural clearing surrounded by rocky jungle-covered hills. A considerable number of rather dilapidated tents – roofs only, no sides – were already pitched here, and these we occupied. Food was provided for us by a party from one of the Kanyu camps about a mile away. Rogers, once of Bukit Jalil estate near Kuala Lumpur, was among these cooks. A stream which crossed the track about a quarter of a mile beyond the clearing was our water supply, and below the water drawing point one was able to get a wash. A Japanese notice here, addressed to 'Coolies and Prisoners of War', delimited the water-drawing and the washing zones.

We found there were a number of Volunteers (Federated Malay States) in the Kanyu camp along the road, but I was pretty weary with the march. I was carrying a big pack, with a mattress (light camp-bed type) blanket and pillow tied on top; the big fishing bag which I had bought in Melbourne, crammed with possessions which I was anxious to keep; a haversack, likewise crammed and heavy; and a water-bottle – altogether quite a substantial burden – and I did not feel energetic enough to do the extra two miles to see people in Kanyu. I regretted this afterwards as I heard that Harry Malet was there.

Next morning (30 April) off at dawn again, past the Kanyu camp, where I caught a glimpse of Lieutenant-Colonel James and Sergeant Kemp inside the gates, and on through the jungle – high trees and thick undergrowth –

to end up, in the early afternoon, in a camp of bamboo huts in which a detachment of Australians were living. The camp was rather squalid, but the Australians had ingeniously constructed excellent 'showers' by running out bamboo pipes from a spring on the hillside; standing under the spout of cool water one got a very pleasant wash. Sergeant Shearman developed malaria here and early next morning I had a terrific argument with the Korean 'medical' corporal over the question of what should be done with him and the other two or three men who had now become sick and unable to walk. Kanehara shouted and raved in the usual way when I said they could not walk, repeating 'All men must march,' and 'No lorry,' time and again.

Finally, however, the Japanese sergeant in charge of the whole party turned up and quietly indicated that the sick men could wait behind in the camp until a lorry was able to bring them on. This sergeant was quite an exception among the Japanese, and throughout the march behaved reasonably when we were able to get hold of him to make requests about the sick. So off we went again in the early light, through teak and bamboo jungle, up and down over rocky ridges and soft earthy slopes; here and there spectacular trees, covered with a mass of mauve flowers, made a striking contrast with the usual heavy greens of the forest. All along this part of our route we saw orchid clumps on the high branches of the trees, orchids of all shapes and sizes, mauve, blue, yellow and chocolate brown.

In the afternoon we reached Kinsaiyok camp, having in the last part of our journey dropped down again from the ridges to river level. Kinsaiyok is actually on the river bank. Here we were given an open space in which to spend the night – a depressing prospect, for ominous black clouds were piling up and it was obviously going to rain heavily before long. I found Ross McPherson in this camp, looking after a small hospital under frightful difficulties with almost no drugs and a lot of malaria, dysentery and beriberi. Colonel Mackellar, Goldman and van Langenberg were here. Almost the first person I met was Cecil Lea, who I had heard was dead – I told him this and he said he had heard the rumour himself.

Ross McPherson, whose hospitality was untiring, got my kit under cover in his hut and actually gave me his bed to sleep on while he lay on the floor. He also replenished my supply of boiled eggs for the journey, and provided me with the best meals I had on the march. The rest of the marching party were soaked by the rain, I fear: the Japanese in charge of Kinsaiyok camp issued a special order that none of them should be allowed into the permanent buildings of the camp, which were the only shelter. This order was, however, actually rescinded before nightfall (after the rain had stopped) on representations, apparently, from either Lieutenant Ino or Colonel Yanagida – officers of the POW group, *not* the Kinsaiyok POW group, which is 4 Group – who providentially turned up in the late afternoon. This was a concession: but next morning the beneficiaries were only moderately grateful, for the huts which they had been allowed to go in as darkness fell were so infested with bugs that sleep was difficult. In Ross McPherson's hut I had no such trouble. I had a very pleasant bathe, too, in the river after the rainstorm and before dark. There is a fine cliff on the far bank – I swam across and sat in the sun there for a bit.

Next day was a longish march, from Kinsaiyok to Rintin. Rintin had a few huts of bamboo, but very few inhabitants. It had been a Dutch camp,

River and hills at Takanun

but they had had a lot of very severe illness (and I think had been very savagely treated) and 135 of them had died. Most of the survivors had gone elsewhere. On arrival here we were able to buy coffee from a small 'shop'. This was particularly welcome after a long march in the heat. The only water we got on these marches was before starting and what we could carry in a water-bottle, and of course what we were given at the evening meal on arrival; but altogether it was not a great deal, and in that climate on such a march, sweating all the time, one became frantically thirsty.

Next day we marched on to Hindato, where we encamped for the night in tents beside a small stream. The ground was wet.

The following day (4 May) we trudged on to Prangkassi, where again we slept in tents. The ground here was more open, with a kampong and fruit trees on one side, and a small pagoda on a hill a little way off. There were a lot of Dutch in this camp. The river was close by and I had a good wash.

On 5 May our route was much more up and down – we were making our way along a steep hillside above the river, and the road plunged and climbed to get past rocky bluffs and to circumvent impossible slopes. The forest was very thick, however, and we got no view during the march. Towards evening we passed through a small village. A native woman who was watching us go past told me it was called Takanun. It had some better-than-average wooden thatched houses, and a police station with notices and a Siamese flag. There was a magnificent flame of the forest tree in full bloom in the middle of the village. Beyond, our road wound through a big orchard area, through durian trees, mangoes, limes, papayas and coconuts. Further on, on a bluff overlooking the river, were the beginnings of a camp and here most of our party stayed. We, the hospital party and the officers, went on next day a few kilometres further up the river, past a Japanese hospital and transport camp to the Takanun headquarters. There was a detachment of Norfolks here living in very squalid tents, with very bad food: in pretty bad shape altogether. The Japanese have some huts. We were given some tents (not nearly enough) and it was indicated to us that this would be our place of residence for some time.

Takanun

Takanun

15 May 1943

We have now been in this Takanun camp for ten days. Already here on our arrival was No. 16 Battalion – chiefly 5th Norfolks; they came up from Singapore six weeks ago. This camp now becomes 2 Group HQ on the river. 16 Battalion have been living under appalling conditions, crowded in ragged leaking tents, with terrible food – nothing but rice and a modicum of what the Japanese say is dried vegetable but looks like dried seaweed. Their cooking containers are inadequate, and about half a pint of tea at the three meals of the day is all the men receive – quite insufficient for men working hard in the sun all day. With the arrival of our parties, things are a trifle improved. We know rather better than these new arrivals from Singapore how to make the best of local conditions and know what to try for in local purchases. Angier, who is with No. 7 Battalion (a good many Gordons – OC is Colonel Stitt) has already made local contacts to purchase extras which are direly needed.

The accommodation for the men in this camp is hopelessly inadequate: the tents are crammed, but still men have to sleep in the open (some prefer to) or under such primitive shelters as they can improvise with bamboo and a little attap and perhaps a groundsheet. They are being hard worked too. They parade after a hasty breakfast about three-quarters of an hour after dawn, and go on to 6 or 7 Tokyo time (to within an hour or two of sunset) bamboo cutting, tree felling, bridge building, embankment building and making cuttings, pile driving and so on, all in blazing sun under constant pressure backed up by violence. Pemberton, who was here when we arrived, had already warned the Japanese that in the absence of a better diet for workers there would be a breakdown. The sickness in 16 Battalion in these six weeks has become alarming – 240 out of 400 are unable to work now. Many are desperately ill with dysentery, beriberi and pellagra, malaria and exhaustion.

The 'hospital' is supplied with five Japanese tents with mosquito curtains which are squat and low, about 12 feet wide and 15 feet long, and three small leaky Indian-type tents which are smaller but slightly higher. There are no floorboards.

There are a number of Dutch in the camp, mostly Eurasians, whose insanitary habits fill us with dismay, with dysentery so prevalent and flies so numerous. We are having about four deaths a day at present. Desperately sick men are brought in from time to time from neighbouring small camps where there are no British medical officers or orderlies. These men have been kept without attention for so long that when they get here there is nothing to be done except see them die – they are so far gone that there is nothing for us to work on in attempting to save them.

The Japanese are having a 'speedo-speedo' – driving all possible men out to work, ruthlessly cutting down the numbers of people available to do water carrying and cooking, and as often as not refusing to allow us a single man or spade for the needs of camp sanitation. The shortage of latrines is appalling and the condition of the camp and surroundings consequently frightful. The Nips keep demanding more men for the railway and launch furious tirades against us because there are so many sick.

So we live, lying at night on the bare ground or on a hastily constructed frame of flattened bamboo, with no lights, our food little beyond rice and this utterly unappetising, and probably dietetically useless, dried 'seaweed'. We are trying to attend to numerous sick with only a few tents, and those leaky, to accommodate them in, and we have in addition extra desperately ill men dumped on us from outside, brought in on Nip orders as if there were a proper hospital here. One is reminded of the face-saving assurance of the Japanese in Singapore when sending unfit men up to Thailand – that there was a 'first-class fully equipped hospital' at Ban Pong, which turned out to be no more than squalid huts knee-deep in mud and floodwater and sewage.

Some thin starveling cattle have arrived here, brought up by the Nips to give us a meat ration. This ration, however, is very scanty – not 4oz per man gross weight including bone and offal – and quite insufficient to relieve the food situation. Eggs are practically unobtainable, though some sugar and tobacco can be bought from passing small barges and canoes.

The country is picturesque: we are closely surrounded by bamboo and big-tree jungle on steep slopes. Across the river, which runs brokenly in a rocky bed with deep pools, rise fine irregular limestone hills. There are rumours of cholera up the river, and bathing (and fishing!) are restricted.

The great event two days ago was the arrival of Colonel Williamson and Skinner with a batch of letters, the first we have had. I had three, one from M——— in India, one from N——— in Australia, and one from Margaret Cameron. Nothing from home – a disappointment. But it is wonderfully cheering to have any letters, and one reads them again and again.

I have been reading Ronald Storrs's *Orientations* – lent me by Ross McPher-son at Kinsaiyok – with great interest. I was amused to read his complaints at not getting any mail for five or six weeks while on a journey from Egypt to Basra via Karachi. These three letters I have just had are the first I have received since February 1942, fifteen months ago.

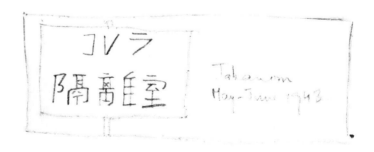

Takanun, 16 May 1943

17 May 1943

I have had two more letters, one, a short one from Mother, the other, rather longer, from Margaret. This is the first news I have had of Margaret's safe arrival in the UK. It brings also the news of RP's death.[1] And a more remote-seeming item, speculation over the filling of the vacant Presidency of Magdalen.

22 May 1943

The conditions in the hospital are really terrible. The few tents are crowded, six or seven people on each side lying on roughly flattened bamboo slats. Most of them are severe dysenteries; they are helpless. There is a lot of rain now, and the tents leak. There is only one bedpan in the whole hospital, and three enamelled pots. The weather is too wet to get the patients outside every day – even if there were stretchers to carry them on – and even if they could be got out we have no soap and cloths to clean the tents up. The stench and squalor of these tents is shocking: what is surprising is how the orderlies manage to keep them from becoming worse. Nursing in any ordinary sense of the

[1] RSH's uncle, Robert Purves Hardie, formerly Reader in Ancient Philosophy at the University of Edinburgh, who died on 9 March 1942.

word is practically impossible. It is no wonder that some of these men despair: last night one of them tried to saw through the arteries of his wrists against a sharp edge of cut bamboo. It's a wonder more don't attempt to do away with themselves. But they need hardly trouble. When they have reached that stage they are almost certain to die anyway.

A lot of medical supplies which were bought at Chungkai and put aside to be brought up here by the Nips for the hospital have been stolen en route. Obviously no proper care of them was taken. The milk has been pillaged from the cases: a lot of sugar has gone and some coconut oil. These things are not all invalid foods but anything that helps to make rice or rice porridge attractive, is valuable.

Most of the desperately sick who are dying are from 16 Battalion – evidence of the conditions of their existence here for the last six to eight weeks.

Max Pemberton has dysentery at the moment, fortunately not very serious. Duncan is bad with his amoebic dysentery again. The anti-malarial party are now almost a permanent fatigue party for the hospital – cleaning the ground, digging drains and making bamboo sleeping floors for the tents. They work very hard. It would be a good thing to do anti-malarial work as there is fresh malaria here but the Japanese have no oil and the hospital work is really more urgent.

A fair number of bedraggled and weary parties of POWs have marched on past this camp further up-river. Occasional parties of Nip troops with handcarts also go by.

We occasionally see a *Bangkok Chronicle* (weeks old), but they give little war news, and devote more and more space to accounts of cultural exhibitions and uplift societies in Bangkok.

I am keeping passably well; and continue to look after the officers' battalion and two of the hospital tents.

23 May 1943

Still raining. There are some cases in the hospital which seem very like cholera – vomiting, watery diarrhoea, cramps, intense prostration and dehydration. With the numberless flies and the continued rain, which effectually prevents airing and cleaning the tents, the hospital is truly a sinister and depressing place. It looks as though we were in for a disastrous epidemic. Latrines are utterly inadequate, and the Japanese demands for workers on the railway prevent us finding men to dig extra ones. The Japanese are constantly demanding that the hospital orderlies do jobs in the Japanese area of the camp, so getting things in order in the hospital is delayed.

26 May 1943

This is cholera all right. There have been 10 deaths already, death supervening within thirty-six hours of the onset of serious symptoms.

The Japanese are much alarmed by this development. Their first step was to have a bamboo fence built between their part of the camp and ours. At the gate is a box, with a folded-up sack soaked in disinfectant, lying in it. Anyone passing into the Japanese area must wipe his feet on this mat. He must also wash his hands in a bowl of disinfectant alongside.

A site on a rough slope outside the present hospital area, and separated from it by a small ravine, has been designated by Colonel Yanagida and Nobusawa as the place where three tents, which they will give us to accommodate cholera cases, will be pitched. They have already given us one extra tent for suspects.

If a man in the main camp contracts cholera, the other occupants of his tent are quarantined – they don't go out to work and are confined to a small area but are available for jobs about the camp. By this means we have got men to dig some new latrines. But it needed a cholera epidemic to do it.

Bathing in the river has been stopped.

All purchases from Siamese boats and barges, even of eggs for cooking, have been prohibited.

The whole camp is to be inoculated with cholera vaccine. A Japanese pathologist from the laboratory a few kilometres down-river was here a couple of days ago. He said he had identified the vibrio in specimens. He seemed to know something of his subject.

The Nips, it will be seen, are doing everything to prevent the spread of the cholera. They have done nothing at all for the men who get it. De Wardener is trying to organise a supply of saline for intravenous administration, but there are great difficulties.[1]

Today has been the first fine day for some time, and we have been able to get our bedding dry again. We have moved our tent a little further over towards the river, overlooking a bend, a pleasant outlook. Cooking, which had become a little more varied before the cholera broke out, thanks to purchases of sugar, soya bean and some frying oil, has been restricted again to rice and stew, to give as little chance as possible to flies to spread infection by contaminating incompletely covered food. The river has risen a good deal and is very turbid. The epidemic, however, has resulted in the cookhouses getting another filter-pump from the Japs and the hospital has been given a 40-gallon drum for water. Besides building new latrines the quarantined men are levelling the ground where the cholera tents are to go up.

29 May 1943

56 cholera cases so far, of whom 21 have died. There are still a number of very severe dysentery plus beriberi plus malaria cases. The new cholera site has been completed and the tents pitched: they are in fact already occupied. The river is rising.

1 June 1943

The total of cholera cases is now over 80, with 35 deaths. One of them was Lieutenant Cole of the Malayan Civil Service. Another officer who has died is Lieutenant Evans. He died last night of cerebral malaria. So did two other men in the hospital. Rain is falling almost continuously and it is not possible to do anything without getting soaked. The tents leak abominably – and there are quite a number of men who have not even tents to cover them. We are told that more tents are coming; meanwhile all we have had is a pep talk

[1] Note by RSH. He did, however, succeed quickly in the face of very real problems and there can be no doubt that this was a life-saving achievement.

by the Jap colonel, translated by Adachi, to the effect that although the country is beautiful it is unhealthy and we must look after our health.

One of the chief troubles as regards diet in hospital is that when a man is very sick – particularly in bowel complaints – there is almost literally nothing that we can give him. There is very little milk, and tapioca flour is monotonous and unsustaining: but I suppose it is really the great standby of the dysenteries, flavoured with sugar.

2 June 1943

The rain goes on – the monsoon in full blast. In the mornings mist wreathes and smokes along the hillside above us, green with its feathery bamboos and tall trees. In the soaked stillness of the air, out of the wet woods, come occasional plangent and fluty bird notes. It is wet, wet, but rather impressive and beautiful.

7 June 1943

A lot of rain still. The river has risen over ten feet in its wide bed and is swirling down in a steady yellow rush, submerging the willow-like bushes along the banks, and carrying down on its surface great matted tangles of trees and bamboos. The cholera epidemic is now tending to abate. Let's hope the anti-cholera measures will also reduce dysentery.

Fit men are going to be moved out of the camp to a new one which is to be built half a kilometre or so above this. This, we are told, will be left as a hospital camp.

Purchase of extra foodstuffs is still altogether forbidden. Our rice ration is being cut down from over 20oz to about 17oz daily. If we got anything else as well to speak of, 17oz would be enough. The Japs say the reason for this is that the rain has made transport very difficult. But the rising of the river has made it possible for barges to get up here easily now.

Yesterday a very forlorn party of prisoners straggled past our camp. They had marched, they said, from Ban Pong (over 200 kilometres) and were not sure how many days they had taken over the journey. Their food had been nothing but rice, with a soupçon of vegetable. They have had no shelter at night, have had to bivouac by the roadside, in all this monsoon rain, which soaks them equally by day. They were evacuated from Changi as unfit, going to Siam to a 'convalescent camp'; but when they reached Ban Pong they were turned out of their train and sent off on this terrible march. The casualties among these unfortunates are already high, and will go higher, for they are exhausted and without reserves.

I have started using some oral quinine HC1 tablets for intravenous administration. The solution seems to work quite well. I am restricting its use to cerebral or other very severe malarias, as I have only the one bottle of HC1 tablets.

13 June 1943

The abatement in cholera incidence is continuing. But other camps, we hear, are having it. The building of a bamboo and attap hut for the hospital has now begun. There have been long fine intervals in the last two or three days.

I have been having malaria – benign tertian obviously. This is my fifth day of quinine. I never had the typical ague or shiver. The first night curious cold crawling chills played up and down my spine. The headache and bone ache were severe – and of course a bamboo bed is not very comfortable even if one is well. Sweating so much, it is hateful not to be able, on account of the weather, to get one's bedclothes dry. Quinine makes one deaf, and one has a peculiar feeling of 'apartness' – particularly during the nights, which seem uncannily silent. I am beginning to eat again now.

17 June 1943

Pantellaria and Lampedusa are said to be in our hands. We seem to be on the eve of great events.[1]

I am returning to duty and hope to get on with some anti-malarial work. There is obviously a lot of fresh malaria here.

The cholera epidemic is abating, but men are still dying from the after-effects as there is practically no food available which they can assimilate. Men are also dying of dysentery and malaria and food deficiencies of course.

The Japanese pathologist who has been around in connexion with the cholera has shown himself quite sympathetic: but he has no medical supplies and cannot do much for us. A Japanese medical colonel who came to visit the camp and actually made an inspection of the hospital area is understood to have said, 'These conditions are terrible.' But still we receive no medical supplies, no emetine, no iron (anaemia is everywhere) and practically no bandages or dressings. We manage to get enough quinine from the Japs, largely by misrepresenting the numbers of men in the camp who have malaria – I give them a grossly inflated figure. The weather is rather tending to improve.

19 June 1943

There are rumours that when this section of the railway is completed we are to be sent elsewhere 'for a rest'. One story is that some will go to Indo-China, some to Bangkok, some to Burma and some to North Malaya. Other 'authorities' say we are going to Formosa. We have heard by roundabout routes that some parties have been sent from Singapore to Borneo. Another story is that the Thai government has asked the Japs to take us away, as they are afraid of being held responsible afterwards by the British government. Unlikely, one would think.

23 June 1943

I am feeling pretty well again. Cholera has disappeared from this camp, though some of the men who have had it and are unable to pick up – it is a frightfully

[1] Note by RSH. My diary does not record news obtained from our secret wireless receiver, as I feared lest this might lead to trouble if the Japs should somehow got hold of my diary and read it – most unlikely of course but there was no justification for taking chances. If I do record an item of news it was generally obtained either from a Siamese newspaper or from some Japanese soldier. Later on, in 1944, the possession of even Siamese newspapers was forbidden and severely punished.

Takanun. (VI Bn camp)

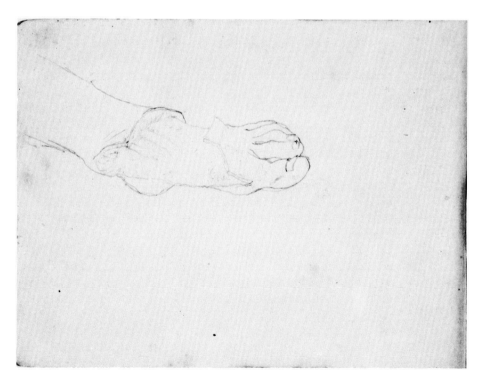

Opposite and top: Takanun. Bottom: Tropical ulcer

severe and prostrating illness – are still dying more or less of exhaustion. Occasional cases of cholera come in from surrounding camps.

The troops – and particularly perhaps the officers' battalion – in the 'fit' camp a little bit up-river from here are being driven extremely hard by the Japanese engineers, who see their slave manpower dwindling away with ill-health. They are paraded at 7.30am (5.30am sun time) when it is just light – so they have to get their breakfast in the dark if at all – and do not finish till 9pm. A Japanese colonel is said to have expressed the view that not much more work could be got out of the troops up here. They are certainly going down in large numbers with various forms of disease: so the Jap engineers, who do not regard ill-health as a reason for not working (at least among the slaves), are working the remainder harder and harder as time gets shorter and they feel less certain of getting their railway finished by the date aimed at. Violence to men working is on the increase here and at camps further up. Food is somewhat improved, though elsewhere it appears to be as bad as it could be. A fair number of Japanese barges are coming up now. There are persistent rumours that we are not to be kept here very much longer.

27 June 1943

Our food is now improved – a fair amount of vegetable, as well as a better allowance of meat. This camp consists entirely of sick and convalescent – the 'fit' are up at the working camp not far away. We have had no cholera case for over a week, but some of the men who had it and survived the acute stages are dying now.

The Japs have given us a little diesel oil for anti-fly measures and anti-malaria work. We have found some breeding places not far from the camp and treat them at frequent intervals.

I have been sleeping badly and dreaming a lot – in one dream Margaret showed me a newspaper with a heading 'Swiss do well'. It is rather depressing lying awake at night on a rough bamboo bed a few inches off the damp black soil, which teems with ants, listening to the patter of rain on the leaky tent roof, and the whisper and creak of the bamboo just outside. There is a constant background of sound, too, which one becomes aware of at such times – the shrilling of cicadas, the croaking chorus of frogs, the surge of the river rapids below, the wind in the leaves. For leagues around us lie the wet rocky hills with their dense bamboo thickets and their great forest trees, their rocky cliffs and deep foliage-choked ravines, the sinister and melancholy walls of our prison. Nearer at hand, one thinks of the cholera, beriberi, dysentery and malaria tents with their helpless emaciated occupants lying in squalor, many of them inevitably and despairingly sinking towards death. Sometimes they cry out meaninglessly in their restless discomfort during these long nights; sometimes you hear a weak voice calling for an orderly to attend him, and the short exchange of speech. Then silence again.

The orderlies, incidentally, are doing very well. Sergeant Shearman of the Norfolks has done splendid work among the choleras.

29 June 1943

Yesterday the hospital was visited by a Nipponese medical major, who went carefully round the hospital looking intelligently at the bad cases (and the bad cases are truly appalling). The possibility of evacuation of the sick seemed to be under consideration. Nobusawa notified Duncan last night that he will send him down soon, probably with sick evacuees.

In two days I shall have been in Thailand for a year – and still medical supplies and accommodation for treating the sick are grotesquely inadequate. If it were not that we have gradually become accustomed to the human misery and emaciation in these camps, one's blood would be curdled daily by the sight of the human wreckage lying in helpless exhaustion and starvation in the huts. For these men's bodies have been so ravaged by disease that they cannot now absorb food, even if we had ample supplies of easily assimilated preparations.

2 July 1943

Yesterday, the anniversary of my arrival in Ban Pong, opens the second half of 1943: and one wonders and hopes and longs endlessly for something dramatic to happen that will give us some prospect of release from this wearisome, and perilous, captivity.

The evacuation of sick men from this camp has actually begun. Eighty left yesterday, but Duncan did not go with them. He is having malaria again. The men went off in four barges, not unduly crowded. We got them loaded without any incidents. One wonders how long their journey will take. One can only hope that arrangements will be made to look after them at the camps which they pass. We are not allowed to send fit people with them. We hope to get more people away in the next week or two.

Parties of sick men, in an appalling condition, keep arriving here by barge from further up-river, where conditions are evidently much worse than here – huge sores eating deeply into tissues, exposing nerves, tendons, bones; advanced beriberi, with paralysis; gross oedema or frightful emaciation; constant malaria, with emaciation and desperate anaemia.

3 July 1943

Yesterday Nobusawa ordered a parade of all the sick in the camp who could walk at all. Refusing all information, he selected a dozen men who he said must work. Some of these twelve men were utterly unfit, but they had no *visible* damage, such as an ulcer, or *measurable*, such as a raised temperature – so they were called fit for work and twelve more workers must go up to the working camp and the sick camp figures must go down by twelve. Actually we can avoid the worst consequences of this policy by selecting twelve men ourselves who, though not really fit for work, will not take any serious harm by going up to the other camp. But the situation is very difficult, for men are not easily allowed by the Nips to come down to this camp as sick. They are being worked very hard and very savagely up there – from 7.30am to 9 or 10pm every day. Unfit men just collapse if they are sent up. One is under constant pressure to provide men to work under this Nipponese system: for groups of men are given certain work to do in a certain time. If many go sick in a group, the others have to work all the harder and longer. The officers' battalion are constantly asking me to pass as fit men who can come up to help them. One is torn by the dilemma.[1]

Stories have come down, brought by sick men, of the horrible conditions in British and Australian camps up-river. They are having a lot of cholera, and their daily rice issue is only 7oz per man. An Australian camp is said to have had 100 cholera deaths, a British one 200.

A lot of Tamil, Chinese and Malay labourers from Malaya have been brought up forcibly to work on the railway. They were told that they were going to Alor Star in northern Malaya; that conditions would be good – light work, good food and good quarters. Once on the trains, however, they were kept under guard and brought right up to Siam and marched in droves up to the camps on the river. There must be many thousands of these unfortunates all along the railway course. There is a big camp a few kilometres below here, and another two or three kilometres up. We hear of the frightful casualties from cholera and other diseases among these people, and of the brutality with which they are treated by the Japanese. People who have been near these camps speak with bated breath of the state of affairs – corpses rotting unburied in the jungle, almost complete lack of sanitation, frightful stench, overcrowding, swarms of flies. There is no medical attention in these camps, and the wretched natives are of course unable to organise any communal sanitation.

7 July 1943

Yesterday morning another parade of all sick capable of walking more than a few yards. The parade is held in the Japanese portion of the camp, so as to save Nobusawa from walking more than a few yards. The fact that the sick have to totter over muddy ground, down into a hollow and up again, several hundred yards in each direction, does not strike him as unreasonable.

He divided the sick into two roughly equal groups: one group of sick need not work, all the others were to do 'light work'. You couldn't tell, looking at the two groups, which was which. Nobusawa would not pay any attention to what we had to say about these men. Many of the 'light works' were hobbling with sticks as a result of painful ulcers and muscle weakness from vitamin deficiency. One had renal colic, but no pain at the moment of examination – hence nothing to be seen, therefore fit for work.

Colonel Yanagida was a party to this unedifying performance: he climbed on to his box again and made a speech, translated by Adachi the interpreter. The colonel regretted that there was so much illness: every one must do his best to look after his health. The railway was nearly finished, and soon we would be able to rest.

Lieutenant Hashimoto, the swashbuckling camp adjutant, followed with a noisy Hitlerish speech in Japanese. Everyone must work: malingerers would be punished. The 'light work' would be only half-day work.

One knows by bitter experience that though 'light work' begins by being light work, in a very few days it becomes heavy and full-day work. At Chungkai a similar 'light work' group found itself carrying rice-bags three or four days after being promised by the Japanese only light work. The reason for this is that the Japanese medical authorities apparently cease to have any power of supervision over the administrative side as soon as the men are handed over.

[1]See note by RSH, Appendix.

The administrative side are only interested in getting work done, and it is no one's business to see that they observe the restrictions due to medical considerations.

As a matter of fact today Lieutenant Hashimoto, who has a reputation for being very severe but fair, himself went out with the 'light work' party and saw to it that they did their 40 minutes work, 20 minutes rest, and had extra tea brought for them. He was also reasonable towards those who were too sick to work seriously, sent them back into the camp and in general behaved well.

Since the Japanese gave us some anti-malarial oil, the anti-malarial party have been going out and dealing with breeding places around the camp – we have found quite a lot. It is pleasant to get out of the camp and wander along the river banks.

We have been on malaria prophylaxis for some time now – about a month, I think. At first the dosage was one 3-grain tablet per man per day, and one tablet of plasmoquine (0.02gm) once in ten days. I had to put in a return every ten days showing (a) the number of men for prophylaxis and (b) the number undergoing malaria treatment. The two figures amount to the camp total. The quantity the Nips issued was then calculated (a) × 10 and (b) × 5 tablets × 5 days, that being the amount allowed by them for treatment.[1]

Now, malaria continuing to be a major cause of loss of work, the prophylaxis is to be stepped up to two 3-grain tablets on alternate days, one on the other days.[2] So we are at present getting enough quinine for treatment of active cases.

8 July 1943

Duncan Black went off this morning, we gather on his way to Ban Pong. Petrovsky has a story that when the troops leave here we, the medical officers, will be left to look after the coolies. If we are isolated in separate camps, conditions are not likely to be very pleasant.

12 July 1943

Nobusawa, the 'so-called doctor', says British medical officers may be kept on to look after coolies who will be here after the British troops are evacuated. Meanwhile, we are getting on with the evacuation by river barge of the sick who are obviously not likely to be fit for work for some time. Nobusawa makes the selection, as he says he does not trust the British medical officers. Actually, of course, we are most anxious to send the men who need evacuation

---

[1] Note by RSH. In view of the inadequacy of this course I was compelled to inflate the number given under (b) and furthermore, as the prophylactic dose was so inadequate as to be useless, not to issue it for prophylaxis. Similarly I kept the plasmoquine for treatment, as that amount was quite valueless for prophylaxis – plasmoquine is in fact quite useless for prophylaxis in *any* quantity. I did not record these facts in writing in my diary for obvious reasons. However, at this stage this ignoring of the Japanese medical office instructions was not attended by much risk as they did not appear to be in any way suspicious; or perhaps did not care.

[2] Note by RSH. This would make no real difference either, and I continued to withhold prophylactic quinine to a large extent in order to have enough for proper treatment; but the Japanese action indicated that their attention was turning towards interest in the prophylaxis, and I made arrangements for suitable information to be given to them if they made enquiries of the battalions and even to issue the quinine at meal times if any of the Japanese medical office came around enquiring about when it was given out.

most urgently, so his pains are really quite unnecessary. He appears to argue that we would make a 'racket' of evacuation – accepting 'commissions' for putting people on evacuation lists – if he did not do the job. As he does not make a list of the names of the people he selects for evacuation, only makes a note of the total number, we are in a position without difficulty to put those who we think are most urgent on the lists, up to the figure he has decided on. Nobusawa's selections as a matter of fact are often quite reasonable – no one could fail to be impressed by the large numbers of grossly emaciated or anaemic men. But his systematic rejection of men whose vision is failing owing to vitamin deficiency is inexcusable. However, we are getting off quite a considerable number of men.

The morning parades, when these men are taken to the waiting barges, are pitiful spectacles. On stretchers carried by hospital orderlies, or tottering along helped by less disabled comrades, these human wrecks are lined up at dawn on the Japanese parade ground. It is often pouring with rain, but the poor devils are lined up nonetheless, as often as not with more delay than usual, either because the Japanese sergeant who usually comes out to supervise and make a fuss is not up yet, or because the Siamese who work the barges are not ready. Finally, after being counted and the names checked off on the list, the melancholy procession creeps down the steep banks of the river to the little shingle beach where the barges lie, the men are packed in and off they go, out of our ken and, we hope, to a destination where they will have a

Takanun

better chance, if they survive the journey. We don't know under what conditions they make the three to four days' journey down: we fear it must be a desperate business for a number of them. But one doesn't feel justified in refusing to give these men a chance.

Cholera has broken out a few kilometres from here, where a large party of Australians and Burmese are clearing a site for a big coolie camp. They have been isolated, with armed guards, to prevent communication with any other camps.

Today the 'light work' party was paraded at 7.30am. They were put on work as hard as anything done by fit men – pulling heavy logs along a track to where a trestle bridge is being built. (This is usually done by elephants, but the elephants have gone elsewhere.) They have been kept at it, not being allowed back to camp for a midday meal, and are to work till 8 pm this evening. One man who collapsed was left lying in the mud. The Japanese guards refused to allow him to be moved – soldiers who tried at least to make him more comfortable were violently ordered by the armed sentries to leave him and continue their work. He is still out there.

Today also a party of 20 helpless Dutch sick came into camp from up-river – one lad, a Javanese, on the point of death with tuberculosis, another dying of dysentery and so nearly dead that his filthy blanket was already a mass of flies and bluebottles attracted by the stink of putrefaction and death. That the sick have to reach such a desperate condition before they qualify for evacuation shows the extent of the Nipponese recognition of humanitarian principles. The whole party of just-living skeletons, collapsed and exhausted, made a ghastly picture: bearded, filthy, those that could stand staggering with match-stick legs and wasted faces, their eyes glazed with anguish and despair. No protest to the Jap authorities against this inhuman treatment of the sick, and the barbarous brutalities being inflicted by the engineers and guards on the railway workers, seems to have any effect.

13 July 1943

Another 80 men went off this morning, drenched before they started by heavy rain on the dawn parade. Eda shouted and raged over an error made yesterday (and corrected) about ten men not cholera-tested before being listed for evacuation; and about one man whom I had to substitute for Wells, a desperate chronic malaria case who really couldn't be considered fit to start this morning.

17 July 1943

Another 80 men evacuated this morning, making more than 800 already. Nobusawa had another evacuation parade today. It is a great relief to get so many men off, as we know that conditions down at Chungkai are much more favourable than here. The only snag lies in the arduousness of the journey down the river.

At the evacuation parade Nobusawa told Petrovsky and myself, with a grin of triumph: 'Very bad news for you. Germany, Russia, shake hands, fighting finished.'[1]

[1] Note by RSH. Had we not had our radio news we might have felt very depressed by this. As it was, we endeavoured to look seriously concerned.

Today Max Pemberton amputated Barber's leg. Barber had been in one of my tents for a few days with a very deep and painful tropical ulcer at the back of his knee – the burrowing of the process had exposed the sciatic nerve and the popliteal vessels. He's very thin and in rather poor shape. He was very upset when I told him he would have to lose his leg to save his life: but there was no doubt about that. I hope he will do.

21 July 1943

Barber is doing all right – shaky, but steadying. Basil Peacock, who is still at Tarsao, has been in this camp collecting pay. He says Bill Adams has gone to Tamarkan, the bridge camp near Chungkai, which is a convalescent camp. He reports also that there are 8,000 sick at Chungkai, 1,000 at Kanburi and perhaps 1,200 at Tamarkan.

There is a story that 30 British and Australian medical officers specially lectured to in Singapore on cholera and sent up to Siam with hospital equipment (which was taken from them by the Nips as soon as they arrived at Ban Pong) are coming up-river to look after coolie camps.

The conditions in the coolie camps down-river are terrible, Basil says. They are kept isolated from Japanese and British camps. They have no latrines. Special British prisoner parties at Kinsaiyok bury about 20 coolies a day. These coolies have been brought from Malaya under false pretences – 'easy work, good pay, good houses'. Some have even brought wives and children. Now they find themselves dumped in these charnel houses, driven and brutally knocked about by the Jap and Korean guards, unable to buy extra food, bewildered, sick, frightened. Yet many of them have shown extraordinary kindness to sick British prisoners passing down the river, giving them sugar and helping them into the railway trucks at Tarsao. It is evident the evacuees go by barge to Tarsao and by train from there.

The hardships which these evacuees suffer on the way down are great. But we must get them down. The barges reach Tarsao in one day, usually (the men are given two full meals to carry with them when they leave here) but sometimes they stop for the night at Kinsaiyok. They spend the night on the barge – at least they are under shelter, for all the barges are roofed. There are apparently no regular arrangements for feeding the evacuees either at Kinsaiyok or Tarsao, but usually they get some rice before starting next morning. Basil says it is not easy, with the best will in the world, to do anything for these passing parties, as sometimes the Japs will not allow anyone to approach the barges or huts in which the sick men are. At Tarsao they are herded into some huts in the coolie camp isolation area, where of course they have no one to look after them – the less sick men have to do what they can. Occasionally Basil manages to get across to see them, but generally no communication with the outside is permitted to them. Next morning, hungry and exhausted, often wet, they (or those of them who can walk it at all) have to trudge half a mile to where the train is drawn up. Those that can't walk are usually pushed along in wheelbarrows by men from Basil's party, if the Japs don't want them or the wheelbarrows urgently for anything else. In what sort of condition do these poor devils reach Chungkai?

Cholera seems to be occurring in a lot of camps. Longbottom has heard from someone that when the first case of cholera occurred at Kinsaiyok the

Japanese military commandant was much alarmed and said that the man (a British soldier) must at once be shot and buried. It was stated that this order was actually carried out by Koreans, and that an enquiry into this is being held at Tarsao.

A similar story comes from another camp. A British soldier working on the line was so savagely beaten by a Japanese guard that after seven days' unconsciousness he died. The British medical officer made out the usual death certificate, and gave the cause of death as 'Murder'. No comment was made by the Japanese office to which the certificate went. Our own experience here is that the Japanese alter our death certificates if they don't like them.

'George' Robey has heard from someone that at the Kanyu camps, where conditions have evidently been extremely bad, Harry Malet, Bellingham Smith, Tacchi and another Volunteer have died.

There are rumours that a big camp for prisoners of war is being built near Bangkok.

Some men of an anti-aircraft regiment who have come to Tarsao from Indo-China, especially Saigon, are much shocked by POW conditions in Siam. They report much local sympathy among Annamese and French; and complete inactivity in the port of Saigon. They themselves were treated well by the Japs in Saigon. They were engaged, at one time, in unloading ammunition from a hospital ship.

The railway is said nearly to have reached Kinsaiyok now.

From what we can hear, our No. 2 POW Group has on the whole had a better time (bad though it has seemed to us) than the other groups on the river. These have, it appears, had higher casualties and more cases of violence and brutality.

22 July 1943

Evacuation of the sick has temporarily stopped. The Japs say that the number of men already sent down to the base camps is more than there is accommodation for and some of those arriving can only be made room for if men sleep in the open. Petrovsky got a fair amount of drugs and dressings yesterday from Sergeant-Major Eda – Nobusawa being away. The stuff was of British manufacture and one wonders where the Japs obtained it.

There was a stir this afternoon when Eda came along to tell us that two Japanese medical officers had been up at the working camp, asking troops if they had been receiving daily quinine. Eda said the troops replied in the negative. He added that he thought that very few men were getting it. This may be true at the working camp, but conditions there make complete distribution almost impossible – the men go out to work before light and come back after dark. The camp is muddy and intensely overcrowded. Eda said the Japanese were going to do some Tanret tests[1]. We shall obviously have to watch our step here if we are to avoid trouble over this.

One good thing these Jap officers have done is to lay down a better scale of quinine treatment for cases of malaria. The standard course is to be fourteen days at 18 grains (six tablets) a day, one tablet of plasmoquine (.01 gm) being

---

[1] A urine test to establish the presence of quinine, named after the French physician Charles Tanret.

given in addition on the last five days. Prophylaxis may be raised to 6 grains (two tablets) per day.

Barber, who had his leg off, is coming along well, though a bamboo bed is hardly comfortable for him.

The Japanese have issued to me a pair of cheap rubber and canvas boots (too small to wear) and a pair of coarse grey calico pants. These are the only items of clothing I have had from the Japs, and since August last they have, they say, been making a deduction of 15 ticals per month from my pay. So I have paid 180 ticals for these two items.

More stories filter in about the coolie camps, where, at least in some, British medical officers are working. Before a coolie can report sick at all to the British medical officer he must obtain permission from the Japanese guards, who do not of course often give it. Even when he sees the medical officer, generally very little can be done for him, as the medical officers are not supplied with drugs or dressings. But at all events the man goes into the hospital hut, where what can be done for him is done. He stays there for as long as necessary, or until the Japanese guards think it time that the hospital cases should be weeded out – by them. The medical officer has no authority.

Men with cholera are taken out to makeshift shelters in the jungle and left there. If they have friends who will look after them, these do what they can. If they have not, so much the worse.

A fatigue of officers at Kinsaiyok goes each morning to the Tamil lines and carts away for burial anyone who has died during the night.

29 July 1943

Another 50 sick men evacuated from here this morning. They left at 10am without any fuss or shouting from the Japs. (Nobusawa is still away.) There have been a few more cases of cholera in this camp, due no doubt to the recent arrival of nomadic prisoner parties from Kinsaiyok, Tarsao and other places.

Jim Adams, Martens and John Russell, with their telegraph line party, are in a camp two kilometres below here. Adams looks pretty ill – he was here today. The food they are getting is very bad. They get practically nothing but rice and dried vegetable. The Japanese party with which they are working sometimes kill an ox.

There are about 100 Japs to 350 British. The prisoners receive the head, the lights and the bones. The Japs take all the rest. The prisoners in this party are being hard worked, with long hours. They have no time to wash or rest and are worn out; whenever they have finished wiring a section they have to strike camp and move on to the next place. They have simply had to leave their choleras and other seriously ill cases behind – if possible in local POW camps – but sometimes they are not able even to get into communication with the camps to tell them they have left a man at such and such a place. They do not know what happens to these unfortunate men.

Adams and Russell, who have been at Kanyu, confirm the terrible conditions there and that Harry Malet, Bellingham Smith and many other Volunteers died.

The Nips there refused to recognise malaria as an illness. They forced men out to work with fever on them, and many collapsed on the railway trace. They had nothing like enough quinine. There had been 70 deaths in three days between Russell's and Martens's visits there.

1 August 1943

I am having malaria again. No particular news. An officer working on the railway was knocked unconscious with a heavy bamboo by a Nip who did not think he was working hard enough.

4 August 1943

Tom Douglas tells me that he knows definitely that Beeley of the Rubber Research Institute, Kuala Lumpur, died at Kanyu.

A British bombardier, Royal Artillery, who has arrived at this camp after being in a POW party cooking for the droves of Tamil and Chinese labourers being marched up the river under guard to work, told me this morning of the terrible treatment these poor wretches get from the Japanese. Many are contracting cholera; often of course it is quickly fatal, but if there is any delay in a man's dying the Nips try to get the British POWs to bury them before they are dead. On one occasion they forced them at the point of loaded rifles to lay them in shallow graves; but the British (they were only a handful of other ranks, no officers) steadfastly refused to do any more. The bombardier reported that the Japanese themselves – terrified as they are of going near cholera cases – covered the bodies. Other dying men were taken out into the jungle and dumped there to die, the Nips compelling other coolies to do this at the point of the bayonet.

At another camp a tentful of sick and helpless coolies was left behind in heavy rain, the Nips compelling other coolies to remove the tent from over them before leaving. At Rintin, the bombardier said, helpless coolies as well as dead were carried on stretchers to the cemetery and all dumped there among the old crosses. He said he himself had seen one old Indian struggling to his knees before a cross and holding up his hands in prayer before collapsing. He says that at Kinsaiyok men are sometimes compelled at the point of the bayonet to brain coolie cholera cases with a hammer. At all the camps cholera cases are treated as untouchable (except by British POWs, who are heavily sprayed with disinfectant before they are allowed to approach the Nips again), and the permanent camps which are sometimes quite near are not allowed to do anything for the wretches. There is no one to give them water. They are left to rot, their bones a memorial to the arrival of the New Order and a comment on the attitude of the Japanese to their fellow Asiatics of other races. When one hears of these widespread barbarities, one can only feel that we prisoners of war, in spite of all the deaths and permanent disabilities which result, are being treated with comparative consideration.

Parties of British POWs are passing this camp today on their way up-river. They have left here a good number of sick, mostly with bad feet. With nothing but broken-down boots or shoes (no socks) on these muddy and rocky tracks, the sodden skin quickly breaks down and ulcerates, and the feet sometimes swell up horribly. Stragglers totter past, often as much as twelve hours behind the vanguard. They confirm the terrible conditions among the Tamils. They often come across dead bodies along the jungle tracks.

Takanun, 7 August 1943

16 August 1943

I have now got jaundice. Thank goodness nothing worse, but it is a most uncomfortable and prostrating condition.

18 August 1943

Unable to shave for a few days. I find my beard is half grey – a sobering thought. I have recently memorised the whole of *The Scholar Gipsy* and Keat's Nightingale Ode.

23 August 1943

My jaundice is clearing slowly and I feel much better. I am very lucky to be in a camp where there are a good number of medical officers, as I have been able to take a rest. Parties of men are still going past, up-river. We have been notified that a large number of sick from further up will be coming down here shortly, presumably for evacuation.

A Tanret test of a hundred men in this camp showed only 50 per cent positives and there seemed a possibility of trouble, but we managed to argue our way out.

River boat, 16 September 1943

29 August 1943

Nipponese guards made a search of this camp today. They found nothing incriminating except one or two small hoards of quinine. The Nips were inclined to make trouble about this (they say we are selling quinine to the Siamese) but we managed to convince them that the men who had the quinine were newly down from camps further up-river, and succeeded in pacifying them.

13 September 1943

After the search mentioned above, I was afraid of another, so hid this diary temporarily. The alarm has now passed, so I resume it.

The rail-laying party reached this camp six days ago and has passed on upwards. The track is now being strengthened and titivated. Captain Gordon of the Argylls, who walked down here the other day from a camp 10–12 kilometres higher, passed three skeletons and two decaying Tamil corpses on the way.

Food supplies here are better than they were – we get some fresh vegetables and even occasional fruit and eggs.

We have built ourselves a passable hut now to replace our tents. The anti-malarial party did most of the work. We have room for separate bamboo beds, and even tables and shelves.

The nights are getting cooler now. My thin cotton blanket is now very worn and flimsy. But many of the men have none, some lost, some stolen, some sold to Siamese: there will be serious trouble when December and January come.

There is a rumour that a further 1,000 men are to be evacuated from this part of the line.

Troops have landed and are fighting in Italy and the Russians are attacking Kiev.

26 September 1943

Evacuation has started again – 40 men left yesterday, and 103 at midday today.

29 September 1943

A lot of very sick men are coming down from 211km camp (this is 205km) in a shocking condition – gaunt spectres of men, riddled with malaria and food deficiencies. One can do very little for these people. They can't assimilate the sort of food we have except eggs, of which we have very few.

The canteen here (it has recently started and is controlled by a Japanese-Siamese consortium) is running a racket. The Japanese have strictly forbidden us to purchase direct from river boats, which sell sugar in 4-gallon tins for 14 ticals. The canteen makes us pay 21 ticals. Similarly tobacco: what we could buy for 20 cents on the river bank we now have to pay 45 cents for at the canteen.

Chapman, a soils chemist from Malaya, has started a laboratory in a tumble-down attap shed near our hut. He is concentrating at present on yeast preparations with rice polishings as a source of Vitamin B, which is the main vitamin deficiency in our diet.

3 October 1943

The wind for the last few days has been definitely easterly, and the weather is much drier. An officer who has come down from up-river reports over 1,000 Tamil deaths in a coolie camp not far from here.

I have two TB cases in my ward, one of whom will die soon. He is quite unfit to travel with the evacuation parties.

I had a note from Ian at Chungkai the other day. He reports that Nigel Wright, who was reported dead earlier on, is alive and though not well is improving. He is at Kanburi. Harry Malet, Bellingham Smith and George Reason are dead, and so is S. J. Clarke, whom I saw at Wampo on the way up here.

13 October 1943

Now that the camp population has been reduced to less than a thousand, most of the seriously ill having been evacuated, there has been a drive for more men to work on the railway. Hospital orderlies have been put to work on the line and the anti-malarial party has been reduced to two. Sanitation and

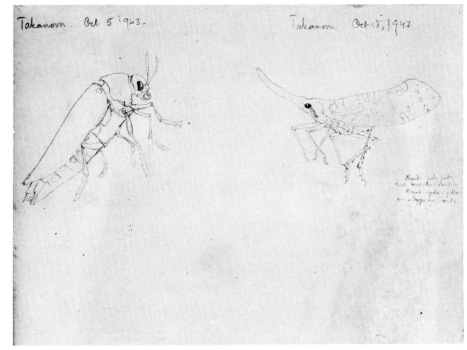

Left: Buprestid beetle, *sternocera sp.*, Takanun, 5 October 1943. Right: Lantern fly, *pyrops sp.*,
18 October 1943

Takanun camp, 16 October 1943

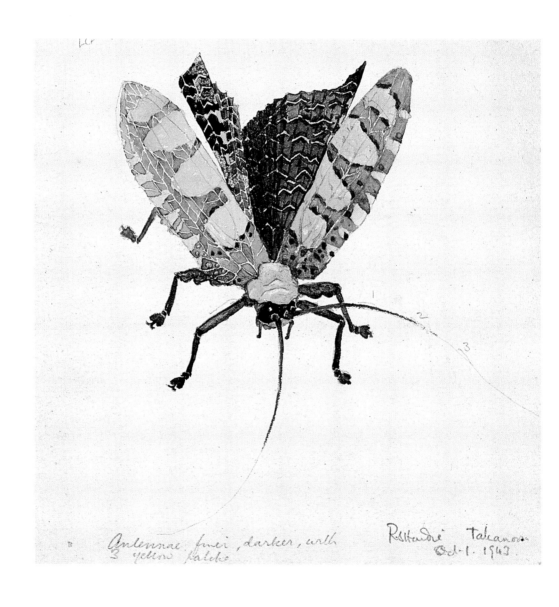

Antennae finer, darker, with
3 yellow ?aloe

Rittadré   Takanon
Oct-1. 1943.

114   Bush cricket, *sanaa imperialis*, Takanun, October 1943

River and hills at Tarsao, 1943

camp police details are cancelled. Sergeant-Major Eda (Nobusawa has gone to Bangkok for two weeks' leave) is making sure that the hospital party are not under-worked.

The weather has been brilliant – north-easterly wind, hot sun, fine starry nights and heavy ground mist in the mornings. The river is falling rapidly and barge traffic must come to an end soon.

Last night, under Sergeant-Major Eda, a party of the hospital staff were marched down the railway to a Japanese HQ camp about three kilometres away

Orchid, *dendrobium eriaeflorum* Griff., Takanun, 2 October 1943

to hear a Japanese military band, which is travelling up the railway giving performances here and there. It was a fine moonlit night. In a clearing surrounded by trees near the camp buildings, mats were laid over a biggish expanse of ground in front of a roughly built bamboo bandstand. (The Japs are good at this sort of construction.) There was some western music – selections from *Carmen* and *The Merry Widow* – and a good deal of Japanese music with its characteristic cadences.

A motley collection of Japanese, Siamese, Tamils and British POWs sat or lay on the mats and listened, while the moon rose from behind the trees into a clear starry sky. The hit of the evening was a war piece by a Japanese composer – *The Air War* – a terrific hullabaloo of drums, wailing sirens, thunderous crashes and aero-engine noises from the strings. Banzai! Banzai! The concert was a pleasant change, and the walk back to camp along the moonlit railway track through the forest was cool and refreshing.

22 October 1943

The first steam engine, pulling two goods trucks and whistling like mad, passed here today, going up. It crept slowly over the trestle bridge near our camp; the bridge groaned and creaked, but stood the strain.

Another evacuation of about 90 men was arranged today; but only 60 got away in the end. The whole party – mostly pretty sick men – was paraded at midday by Jap orders and lined up to wait on the sandy beach where the barges lie; some of the men were helpless on stretchers. The barges to take them downstream were not there 'yet'. The men had to wait in the sun at the river's edge until they should turn up. Two barges turned up after more than two hours. The Japs compelled the last 30 men to wait four more hours until they decided no further barges would be coming; then the 30 men were permitted to creep back or be carried back to hospital. This sort of example of Japanese lack of any attempt at consideration of the sick is now so much a commonplace that we hardly notice it.

I am reading *Anna Karenina* – a poor translation, I think, but an enthralling book.

25 October 1943

A small train went through yesterday with some truckloads of high Nipponese officers sitting on chairs in open goods wagons specially rigged up with carpentered frames carrying attap roofs. They are said to be going up for the ceremony which is to be held at the linking of the rails which have been laid from near Moulmein on the other side, and those laid up this side of the divide. Going out with the anti-malarial party yesterday, I saw that a high screen of fresh-cut bamboo branches had been put up along the railway side where it passes the unbelievably squalid coolie camp a kilometre down the line from here. This is presumably to conceal the camp from the exalted officers on the

'Straggly flower stalks (? shade)
? Shrub - Takanun - Nov 24/1943
- 2-4ft high - here slightly reduced.
Flower more vermilion, clearer colour
? Convolulaceae   Plumbago

Plumbago, *indica coccinea*, Takanun, November 1943

x 1½

RSHaide . Takanoon . Dec 1 1943
Shrub 3-4 ft. ? Hibiscus .   Malvaceae .

Hibiscus, *urena lobata*, Takanun, December 1943

Scenes at Takanun, October 1943

train. But it can't cut off the stench.

To celebrate the junction of the rails, the Japanese have given the workers a whole holiday for one day and have made a special issue of extra food – Japanese tinned milk, margarine and fish.

Basil Peacock, up again from Tarsao to collect pay for his party, brought with him a letter for me, dated 28 June last year, which had somehow turned up in Tarsao.

5 November 1943

There is a story that there have recently been two heavy air raids on Bangkok.

I am having trouble with scabies – presumably picked up in the hospital. It is most uncomfortable and interferes with one's sleep.

11 November 1943

Rumours of a coming move elsewhere for us have become more numerous – to Bangkok, to Saigon etc, etc. What seems undoubtedly true is that the railway work will be coming to an end fairly soon. It is said that the coolies will be left to do maintenance work. Today a very fast aeroplane went over, going east, at about 10,000 feet. The Japanese say it was a British plane. A reconnaissance machine?

18 November 1943

The fast plane went over, eastwards, and came back about an hour later today.

A number of steam trains are now going past regularly – those going up carrying Nip troops, horses, guns, packing cases and so on.

The rumour is that we shall be staying here for a bit, possibly over Christmas.

Work on the line round here is much easier now, though it is still, we hear, very strenuous and hard-driven further up. 'F' Force, who went up past us some months ago, are said to have had very heavy losses, 2,700 out of 7,000 already dead.[1] This is a good deal higher per cent than our figure.

22 November 1943

My scabies and septic spots are still troublesome and I've had a little more fever, nothing much fortunately. The nights are getting distinctly chilly.

The river is much down and there are no canteen supplies; rations unsupplementable and very dull.

24 November 1943

'F' Force are being evacuated from Nikki after a terrible time there. Major Wild told George Graham, who saw him on the train on the way down, that he thought their total deaths would be about 50 per cent before they were

---

[1] This contingent, which consisted of 3,600 Australian and 3,400 British POWs, left Changi in April 1943. When the force returned from Thailand a year later only 3,900 men were still alive, a death rate of 45 per cent.

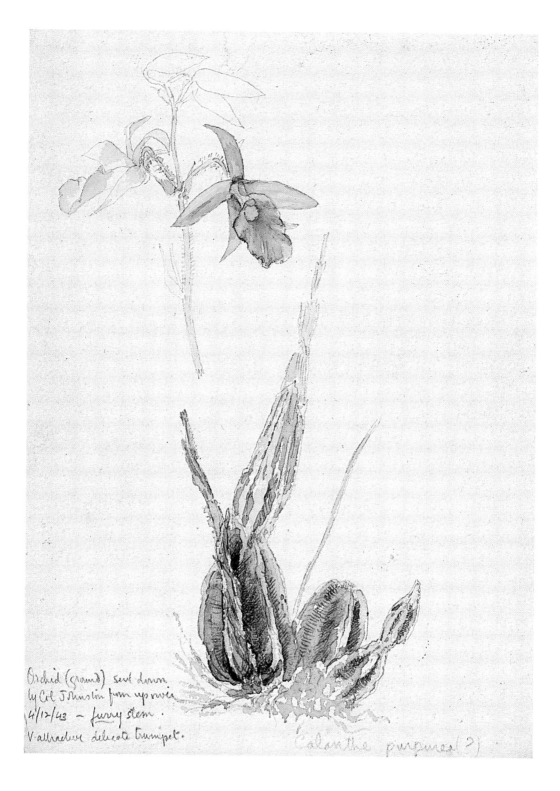

Orchid (ground) sent down
by Col Johnson from up river
4/12/43 – furry stem.
V attractive delicate trumpet.

Calanthe purpurea (?)

Above: Orchid, *calanthe rosea* (Lindley) Bentham, Takanun, December 1943

Opposite: Orchid, *aerides crispa* (Lindley), Chungkai, March 1944

Guards at Takanun, 10 November 1943

finished. Several men had actually died on the train between Nikki and here, and some more were obviously going to peg out pretty soon. The worst sick are still up at Nikki. They must be pretty bad if they are worse than the people on the train whom George saw. This 'F' Force, about 7,000 strong, came up from Singapore last May, and even then 40 per cent of them were unfit; but the Japs in Singapore insisted on their going up to Siam, and said that they were not going to a working camp so it would not matter. They were turned off the train at Ban Pong and had then to walk all the way up to Nikki by jungle tracks, a distance of 260 kilometres. A number had to be left behind at camps on the route; but their guards would not allow more than a few to be left. A British officer in charge of one party which reached Tarsao hunted out a Japanese medical officer there and persuaded him to look at some men in his party who he did not think capable of going further. The Jap actually said 36 men could not march further, and gave a certificate to that effect. But when the British officer took the certificate to the commander of the Jap guards who were conducting the party, the guard commander refused to pay any attention and broke some of the officer's fingers with a heavy bamboo for his insolence in putting the certificate forward. Only six men were allowed to stay behind – the rest had to totter on. The Jap guard commander was of course not an officer, merely an inferior NCO.

Up at Nikki they were treated very savagely by the engineers. Sick men from the hospital were taken out to the line to work – on stretchers if they couldn't walk. Lying on stretchers they could break stones for ballast! Even the Korean guards (and we know something of their ways) were appalled by the behaviour of the engineers. Food was very bad for a long time – watery stew and only about three-quarters of a pint of rice per diem – and there was so much sickness that they got through very little work. Hence the displeasure of the engineers.

The coolies there also had a very bad time. So many were sick that the Japanese one day invaded their camp in force and flogged the sick out with bamboos. A lot of Tamils fled into the jungle and did not come back. The British troops used frequently to find skeletons in the jungle around.

Extra food supplies were almost completely unobtainable. There was a good deal of cholera (200 deaths among the British) and a lot of beriberi, ulcers, diptheria, malaria and dysentery. Practically no medical supplies were issued.

Tarimoto and Kiriama, two notorious engineer officers (they were at Chungkai when I first went there), were at Nikki. They are down on the list.

4 December 1943

Four letters today, two from Mother, one from Margaret Cameron (with news of a godchild on the way) and one from Duncan.[1] Mother's letters dated 21 September 1942 and 15 October 1942, Margaret's 28 September 1942, Duncan's 26 July 1942. They have taken a long time coming.

We are to evacuate another 500 men or so – many of them are not very sick. Chungkai is said to be quite a pleasant camp with excellent food.

8 December 1943

The second anniversary of the Far East War today, celebrated by a special Nipponese parade.

10 December 1943

Nobusawa told Max Pemberton today that a big '10,000 bed' hospital has been built between Bangkok and Ban Pong, to which all bad cases will be sent, while the less bad will be kept at Chungkai.

It is getting pretty cold at night now, with clear skies blazing with stars. People without blankets don't have much sleep. In the hospital we have charcoal fires at night. In the camp a lot of the men spend the night round the fires in the cookhouses.

16 December 1943

A Gordons officer here has heard that of a party of 150 Gordons who went up-river some time ago a hundred are already dead.

A month or two ago, when deaths were becoming infrequent, we had a

---

[1] Husband of Margaret Cameron and brother of Dr Ian Cameron, whose practice in Kuala Lumpur RSH had joined in 1937.

126   Orchid, *dendrobium tortile* (Lindley), Takanun, February 1944

Total length of spray 1ft-8" (15 blooms)

Orchid, *dendrobium gratiosissimum* (Reichenbach f), Takanun, February 1944

memorial service, with Jap permission, in the cemetery. The Japs must have been impressed for today they have 'ordered' us to hold another. We did not understand at first; then we found that there was a senior Japanese officer in the vicinity, so the performance is being put on for his benefit.

There has also been a distribution of extra food – mostly Japanese tinned fish. The tins are to be returned to the Japs after lunch today to prove we have eaten the stuff. Maybe this is also a piece of eyewash to impress the Jap officer, but I for one won't look this gift horse in the mouth.

The quinine we get now from the Japs is all powder – sulphate. No tablets.

18 December 1943

Yesterday, a party of officers, medical officers and anti-malarial people, of which I was one, went down to Songklaburi village to get some canteen stores. Some Jap guards and the canteen manager went with us. We walked down the railway to near where we heard the Jap orchestra, crossed the river in very low dug-out canoes and walked up the sandy bank on the other side into the village. It consisted of two or three short streets of typical two-storey shop houses – the shops open to the street on the ground floor. They were not badly stocked – tinned fish, soap, cigarettes, tooth–brushes, cooking bowls, mats and other commodities. We brought back 2,800 eggs and 100 limes. The village, which is said to owe its existence to a wolfram mine in the hills behind, was quite a surprise in these wild jungles. There was actually electric light in the houses, obtained from a diesel engine and generated in a building on the edge of the village. We bought some quite good coffee with condensed milk at one of the shops. Our Japanese guards were in a good temper, and the whole expedition was a very pleasant affair. Carrying back the eggs and limes in baskets and 4–gallon kerosene tins hung on bamboo poles was laborious, but well worthwhile.

When we returned to the camp, we found that 400 men were standing by to be evacuated. Some of the eggs we brought were just in time to be hard-boiled for them as a haversack ration (one per man). The party had been ordered by the Japanese to parade at 6.30pm but between 6 and 6.30 a train steamed slowly past without stopping. Shortly afterwards, we heard from the Nips, a railway engineer telephoned up from Takanun station, some five kilometres down the line, to say that a train for the evacuees had passed Takanun a little before, but not seeing anybody waiting had gone on. The engineer said that if there was a party to go, they must walk down to Takanun station to pick up the train. It was now dark. This proposal was absolutely typical of the Nip attitude. It would have taken three times as long for the men to get down to Takanun as it would for the train to come back to pick them up. But would the engineers help to that extent? Not they. So as the men were in any case unable to walk, being sick, even our guards agreed that there was nothing more to be done. So the men had to wait for the next train, due about 11pm. There was not likely to be room for more than 150, so 150 were kept waiting beside the line and the others allowed to disband. Finally, at 11.30pm, a train arrived, with only three empty trucks. But 144 sick men were actually packed into these three trucks (we came up to Thailand 26 to a truck and thought it bad enough). I am afraid these men will have a most uncomfortable journey. Fortunately they are not desperately sick.

21 December 1943

The night before last, shortly after 11.30pm, a big aeroplane was heard going south-east overhead. Another and another followed at intervals. Between 3 and 5am they passed overhead again, going back. It was a cheering sound. The moon is in her last quarter.

Yesterday two evacuation parties went off in open trucks – but at least there is no rain just now. They were crammed 46 to a truck in the first party, 56 to a truck in the second – no possibility even of sitting down, except for those round the sides, whose seats would be neither comfortable nor safe. But the men are glad to get away.

One wonders if the shortage of trucks is really so acute. One is inclined to think it is more probable that the engineers who run the trains are, with their well-known perversity, making things difficult and uncomfortable for the prisoners.

24 December 1943

Again last night, about midnight, we heard some big bombers passing over, going south-east. They kept coming back between 2.30 and 5.30am.

Takanun camp. Robert Hardie's hut is on the left, overlooking the river

Work in this camp has been fairly light recently, and Japanese pressure has been relaxed. We are to have a whole holiday tomorrow (Christmas Day) and all sorts of preparations are in progress. There is to be a football match between officers and men, a 'race meeting' on some rough sand and gravel on the river bank, and in the evening a pantomime on an improvised stage facing a high gravel and earth bank. Various strange beers have been brewed, and great efforts in the cooking line are rumoured. The Dutch officers are coming to our hut for a drink in the morning and we go to their party later.

26 December 1943

Yesterday, Christmas Day, was a very remarkable and enjoyable occasion. A great *tour de force* by the cooks, who had been saving things up over a long period, produced a wonderful series of meals in the hospital.

Breakfast, at nine, was rice porridge with lactogen milk; followed by a fried egg, some thick fried pork and fried sweet potatoes; also a tapioca flour roll with a piece of margarine and a good dollop of lime marmalade.

Lunch in the middle of the day was two fish rissoles, following a plate of veg-and-meat soup, two slices of cold beef, some vegetable marrow and some pickles of cucumber and Chinese radish. To wind up, a cup of tea with milk.

Dinner was a veg-and-meat soup; roast beef with fried sweet potatoes and pumpkin; for pudding, a baked ginger pudding and a sauce made with limes; savoury, a sardine on a fried rice biscuit. Dessert, fresh sections of the citrus pomelo; finally coffee with milk.

This sounds as if we were living on the fat of the land. It is true our rations are much better than they were, and we get a certain amount of fresh vegetable. But actually the elaborate menu given above is based on quite a few extras – the Japs allowed us to kill specially for this occasion one pig and one of the cattle. The milk is part of the hospital supply (bought by ourselves) and only the hospital patients were given it. The eggs were bought by ourselves. The fat for frying is mostly purchased by us, not an issue by the Japs. The margarine was some we saved from an earlier Jap issue, to celebrate the completion of the line. The lime jam is made from limes and sugar specially bought by us. The pickles are just part of our ration, in vinegar. Some tins of fish, partly Jap issue, partly purchased, supplied some of the other items. The whole thing was very well done and, though it had involved a fairly heavy levy on our cash, it was worth it. Most of the patients in the hospital were able to enjoy the food. Our parties with the Dutch officers went off well. There was enough drink to produce quite a degree of conviviality, and there was some very hearty singing.

The men won the football match 5–2.

The horse race, with bookies, was passably amusing.

The pantomime *The Babes in Thailand* was a remarkable performance, written and produced by Gus Harffey, with Leo Britt as stage manager. The stage was lit by two Petroma lamps, lent by the Japs – Pycock is very good at borrowing this sort of thing. Sam Flick, 'Ginger' de Wardener, 'Blondie' Clarke, Sergeant Parfitt, Major Woods, Sandeman and RSM Munnoch all did very well; and there was an excellent chorus of brigands. Singing continued far into the night and for a wonder did not lead to any trouble with the Nip guards. One must admit that the Nips allowed a considerable degree of latitude.

And Nobusawa and Sergeant-Major Eda were really quite affable.

Altogether it was a quite remarkably fine celebration for a remote jungle camp miles from anywhere. In the afternoon a party of seven sick men from Hindato came in; it included Staff Sergeant Robertson, who was able to enjoy the Christmas dinner.

31 December 1943

Some letters have come up to the camp. I hear there are some for me, but owing to the Jap interpreter's insistence on reading them (rather absurd, for they are said to be about a year old and have of course been censored by our people) they are being issued very slowly.

A lot of Japanese troops are passing up the line by train now.

This is the last day of 1943, a year to be said goodbye to without regret, holding as it did nothing beyond captivity and depression, weary waiting, and above all the sight of immeasurable human misery, suffering and death.

7 January 1944

Yesterday I got my letters, which have been in the camp nearly two weeks. One of them, from Gwen Desch in South Africa, was written in July 1942. A letter from Margaret (22 January 1943) says they have no official news of me yet. Colin's letter (11 November 1942) is cryptic, but interesting as usual.

A Chinese labourer, with a huge deep sloughing ulcer on his leg, so that he cannot walk at all, is making his way to the coolie hospital camp a couple of kilometres down the line. He gets along seated, lifting himself by his arms – slow progress. The anti-malarial party have been taking him food from time to time. Colonel Williamson, our Indian Army camp commandant, has been asked to put a request forward to the Nips that we be allowed to send a party of officers with a stretcher to carry him down – there is a permanent Jap sentry on a bridge a little below this camp whom it is impossible to pass without authority – but he has refused even to approach the Nips on the subject. The Chinese is a British subject from Singapore. One can't but feel that if it had been a horse or a dog that was in question, he would have been more inclined to approach the Japs. At worst they can only say no.

14 January 1944

Watson, a doctor from Perak, is in the coolie hospital two kilometres down from here. I went down the other day to visit him. He is not able to do much for his sick coolies, as he has practically no medical supplies. He is extremely optimistic about the progress of the war – so much so that when we, the anti-malarial party, feel depressed about things, we propose a trip down to Watson's camp. Lennox, a pathologist, is with him.

The trains going up are numerous and heavy, with troops, horses, guns and all sorts of supplies.

19 January 1944

A soldier with the strange name of Grief was brought into the camp the other

Tamil camp above Takanun, 19 January 1944

day from Prangkassi, with a message from an Australian medical officer that he thought he had cerebral malaria! He was certainly very drowsy, but by the time he got here he had developed unmistakable symptoms and signs of lobar pneumonia (right lower lobe). It's only too likely that he has malaria as well. Luckily we have a little M&B 693 and I have put him on that, with additional doses of quinine by mouth, in case he has malaria. I don't think his 'cerebral' symptoms are due to malaria.

Captain Hodson, a brother of Tom Hodson (whose tea estate at Pandan Aroem near Soekaboemi in Western Java Margaret and I visited in 1939) has come down to this camp from up-river with malaria. He told me that Tom Hodson had had a bad fall on an iron staircase in the tea factory, I think in 1940, had broken one of his vertebrae and had gone home to Ireland, doing well.

20 January 1944

Planes over last night, 1–4am.

22 January 1944

We have been given a postcard to fill up for sending off. We are to give our address as No. 2 Camp, Thailand.

26 January 1944

Archer has come in to hospital from an isolated camp. He reports that when letters came into the camp for them, the Japs in charge withheld the letters from men who were sick and unable to work – they would get them if they worked: otherwise they would be burned.

29 January 1944

Meldrum and Donaldson are to go down to the big hospital camp at Nakom Paton shortly – the camp is not quite ready yet, Nobusawa says.

I saw (Dr) Watson again a day or two ago, very optimistic. He gets hold of the most extraordinary rumours, obviously fictitious, from somewhere, perhaps from Tamils who get them in turn from Siamese. A lot of nonsense today about big operations in Burma. More authenticated accounts of savagery to coolies by Jap guards, crucifixion, drowning, blinding and other atrocities.

16 February 1944

The second anniversary of the capitulation of Singapore yesterday, a melancholy reminder.

A few days ago the Japanese announced that parties would be made up forthwith to go to Japan. Four parties of 150 each are to be arranged with ten officers and four medical officers. The men have all to be certified free from this, that and the other disease. The Japanese are doing blood examinations for malaria – not a very useful proceeding when the whole camp is (supposedly) on prophylactic quinine – inadequate of course to eradicate malarial infections, but probably enough to ensure that the parasites don't appear in the peripheral blood. Longbottom and Petrovsky will be two of the four medical officers to go. Pat MacArthur was chosen but rejected as he probably has amoebic dysentery. It looks as though Ginger de Wardener and I will be the next two victims. Feelings are very divided pro and con going to Japan. There will in any case hardly be 600 fit men in this camp. There is a good deal of speculation as to the dangers of a sea voyage to Japan just now. The groups of 150 are being arranged according to trades (the Japs demand young officers with technical qualifications) so it looks as though they were wanted for work in Japan. It is said that the total number to go from 2 Group will be 1,500 to 1,800. There must be many fit men down at Chungkai now.

There has been a lot of aerial activity at night recently.

Rations are rather poor, but one or two innovations in cooking are helping – notably rice and soya bean bread, and rice and soya bean milk porridge.

I have had news of Emery from an officer who travelled down from Nikki with him, when 'F' and 'H' Forces were going back down-river after their disastrous stay up there. Emery was not very well, but not very ill. The officer confirmed what we had already heard about disease, food shortage and Japanese brutality at Nikki.

I am reading *Vanity Fair* again.

24 February 1944

Of the four parties of 150 for Japan, none of which has left this camp yet, 25 per cent are sick, mostly chronic malaria. The Japs now say that proper blood examinations will be made when the men get down to Kanburi, or possibly Bangkok.

Petrovsky reports that the Japs say we shall all be going down to Chungkai soon, the Japan parties first. Colonel Johnson's and Colonel Swinton's parties have already come down from higher up and are installed in the old Nipponese and Tamil camps four or five kilometres below here. Colonel Johnson has made a remarkably fine collection of orchids, mostly dendrobiums.[1] He has one very striking one in flower at present – I walked down to his camp yesterday – oyster, veined with pink, with two very deep crimson patches on the outer lips of the undermost petal. There is also a fine falling spray, with numerous bright yellow flowers like small yellow pansies.

There was a heavy fall of rain yesterday with a fierce but brief squall of wind.

---

[1] An enthusiastic naturalist, Lieutenant-Colonel AA ('Ack Ack') Johnson grew orchid specimens in a specially built extension to his hut. He also collected butterflies, storing them in old biscuit tins for identification after the war. He encouraged those of his fellow-POWs with artistic talent to draw and paint the flora and fauna of the jungle, helping them to obtain the materials they needed and concealing the artwork from the Japanese.

Chungkai

Chungkai

19 March 1944

About three weeks since my last entry. And now I am right down at Chungkai again, which I left over a year ago. Our evacuation of Takanun took place quite suddenly: at very short notice we were bundled into trains and came down here. I left with a party of hospital evacuees, not seriously ill, at 8.30pm on the evening of 29 February and nineteen hours later we reached Chungkai. The journey was slow and uncomfortable. My party of 28 was packed into a single open goods truck, together with four Nips and one of their bicycles. Condensing steam and cinders from the engine poured down on us as we went along. We got filthy, wet and had holes burned in our clothes. But in general the journey was uneventful. I lost my hat – the papier-mâché topee I bought in Singapore after the capitulation – which fell overboard when I nodded with my head leaning over the edge of the truck as we trundled down through the Tonchan area.

We have been kept nominally apart from the main camp here – we sleep and are counted as a separate group – but we have free access to the whole site. I have attached myself to the hospital laboratory where Ian does blood slides and amoebiasis examinations.

The camp is now enormous, with a very large hospital area. The original hospital buildings, in the putting up of which Duncan Black and I were concerned, are still the HQ of the hospital. Colonel Dunlop,[1] an Australian surgeon, is OC Hospital and a first rate man. He belongs to a group which went from Singapore to Burma and have reached here from the Moulmein side. There are also a large number of 4 Group people, which includes a lot of FMS Volunteers, many of whom of course I know. I usually spend the evenings over at Ian's hut, where John Daly, Hajji Marsh, Max Webber, Beautement and others congregate for conversation. There is a very good canteen, run largely by Volunteers. Colonel Riches is in supreme (nominal) charge: Hare runs the show with the assistance of Clarkson and Woodward. They produce very good extra dishes, stews, omelettes, soups, cakes, toffee-fudge (coconut, peanut and ginger) cigarettes, sambals and coffee. If one has money one can live very well. There is quite pleasant, if not very hygienic, bathing in the river. Existence is altogether more peaceful and pleasant than in the wilds at Takanun: my sleeping quarters in a big hut with the rest of our up-country party are, however, hot, crowded and infested with bugs.

[1] Later Sir Edward Dunlop, Consultant, Melbourne Hospital, Australia.

2 April 1944

There is a small bamboo and matting stage in the corner of this camp, where they have shows and concerts from time to time – there are a number of musical instruments in the camp supplied by the Red Cross. Yesterday there was an excellent performance of Somerset Maugham's *The Circle*, with 'Fizzer' Pearson, Nigel Wright, Gus Harffey, Griffith-Jones[1] and Bobby Spong. The first Japan party left some days ago, we thought for Ban Pong, but they have fetched up at Non Pladuk, and we have word there from Longbottom and Petrovsky. I have been feeling particularly well lately. Martin Finegold has been looking after our cookhouse and doing very well indeed.

10 April 1944

A party of 300 is to go up to 'Burma' again. Major Read is going with it. He has not been up-river as yet. With the monsoon again imminent, it is to be hoped that they will get adequate food, medical supplies and accommodation wherever they are going. Many of the party are chronic malarias. The Japan party at Non Pladuk (they have been there only three weeks) are already showing signs of vitamin deficiency – their food has been very bad and they have been unable to purchase supplements.

There has been aerial activity here, both at night and by day. The anti-aircraft guns at the big bridge over the 'other' river at Tamarkan loosed off ten rounds yesterday at some high-flying bombers.

20 April 1944

My financial anxieties have been removed for the time being by a generous loan of 50 ticals from Bill Adams and by the sale of my cuff-links for 35 ticals. Chapman, the officer in charge of the Japan party which is at Non Pladuk, reports that conditions there are better. Some earlier Japan parties formed from 3 and 6 Groups have, he believes, already gone east via Bangkok, Aranya Prades and Pnom Penh to Saigon, and he expects to follow them shortly.

22 April 1944

This morning Major Read with 200 men went off to 'Burma'. The party had been informed by the Nips that they would be away only 45 days and would then be brought back.

Two nights ago, the hospital HQ hut in which the laboratory is situated collapsed in a sudden wind-and-rain storm. The Japanese have decided that from now on the laboratory will work in the Japanese hospital offices. This is inconvenient and uncongenial.

There is a rumour that the 4 Group people in this camp are shortly to be moved to the main 4 Group camp at Tamuang, between Kanburi and Ban Pong.

---

[1] Later Sir Eric Griffith-Jones QC, Attorney-General and Minister for Legal Affairs, Kenya, and Chairman of The Gunthrie Corporation Limited.

R. B. Perkins, Chungkai, April 1944

4 May 1944

The Japan party at Non Pladuk is still there. The second (Takanun) Japan party is still waiting here – this is Gibson's and Rhodes's party. Further parties for 'Burma' are being made up. There has been some critical comment on the selection of men for these 'Burma' parties – the authorities have not been sufficiently careful to ensure that only reasonably fit men are nominated. This is absolutely vital, for we know that conditions up-river will almost certainly be extremely tough. I believe the nominations are being looked into by HQ to make sure that unfit men are not being sacrificed in the interests of dodgers who want (not of course unnaturally) to remain behind.

8 May 1944

The bridge anti-aircraft guns had a shot or two today at a high-flying recce plane – they got nowhere near of course.

John Daly has gone into hospital with amoebic dysentery. He looks wretched. He quite recently had a broncho-pneumonia, is very thin and far from strong. Peter Shearlaw is also pretty ill with amoebic dysentry, possibly a hepatic abscess.

4 Group are now being moved to Tamuang. Their sick go first – are going already – in groups of 90 to 110 daily by barge. There are about 1,000 'heavy sick' in 2 Group here who are to go to the big hospital camp at Nakom Paton between Ban Pong and Bangkok.

15 May 1944

Poor old John Daly died early this morning. I saw him yesterday and he looked very bad. He was very depressed, and the discomfort and humiliation of our existence had hit him, at his age, harder than most. The severe illness which he went through not long ago had taken the heart out of him, a sad thing when one remembers how courageous and energetic he was during the battle.

A good many of 4 Group have already left this camp – including two leading actors, Pearson and Nigel Wright, and the two leading musicians, Norman Smith and Eric Cliffe. The latter's classical concert last week was very good. They played *Eine Kleine Nachtmusik*, among other pieces.

17 May 1944

A fair amount of rain is falling now – the monsoon is coming on again.

21 May 1944

Leo Britt's musical, *Wonder Bar*, was given last night (when I saw it) and the night before. It was astonishingly good in its way – amazing costumes made out of old mosquito netting, a few pieces of cloth and some dyes. The setting was also remarkably realistic. One could hardly believe it was made out of bamboo, a few pieces of wood and bamboo matting, with some paint of white-wash and local coloured earths. The actors, too, were good and the whole thing reflects enormous credit on the company, the scenery and costume designers, and the producer, Leo Britt.

A fair number of 2 Group 'heavy sick' have left for Nakom Paton. 4 Group are still going off in batches to Tamuang, some by rail: a party of them (some ill men among them) are at this moment, 3.30pm, waiting at the railway side for their train. They have been there since 11 am.

One of the officers on the hospital water fatigue had his jaw broken today by a Japanese, because he was drawing water for the hospital at the wrong

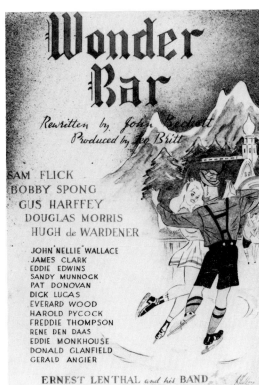

Above and on page 143 : Theatre posters from Chungkai camp

point on the bank.

We have had some mangoes recently, most luscious.

28 May 1944

All 4 Group prisoners have now left this camp and gone to Tamuang.

It is said that the camp, now it has a smaller population, is to be rearranged; the hospital is to be in the three long huts on the extreme east side of the camp area. The huts in which we were put when we came down from up-country will be pulled down and all that area will be taken over by the Japanese.

Some American Red Cross parcels have arrived. There is one parcel between each six men.

Dudley Gotla's stage show, to which he gave the purely nonsense-name of *Thai Diddle Diddle*, has been banned by the Nips. They have given no reason for this. There was nothing in it about the war, or about the Thais. My theory is that the Japanese interpreter looked up the word 'diddle' in a dictionary and finding that it meant 'deceive' or 'cheat' suspected some subtle criticism of the Co-Prosperity Sphere. It is astonishing how tortuous the Japanese are in some ways, and how unbelievably gullible in others.

2 June 1944

Quinine supplies have been insufficient for prophylaxis recently (which doesn't matter) but just sufficient for treatment, with careful management.

The number of mosquitoes in the camp has gone up rapidly lately, on account of the rainwater lying in and around the area. The big anti-malarial drains system outside the camp, which was maintained by the anti-malarial party until the beginning of this year, has fallen into neglect and, although we began making representations a long time ago, the Japanese will not allow any work to be done by the anti-malarial party outside the camp. If we could get permission for a party to go out, we could do a lot to cut down the dangers of another epidemic of malaria such as we had when we first came here. During 1943, when the drains were looked after and oiled, this camp was quite remarkably free from malaria.

The camp population here is about 4,500, among whom there are two parties, of 750 and 500 respectively, due to go to Japan. In addition there are about 500 sick who are to go to Nakom Paton.

7 June 1944

The Japan party of 750, with Lewis and Braham and McNeill, went off today. They are said to be going to Singapore for embarkation. Robson and his party go tomorrow. All these men will leave without their letters, which have been lying 'uncensored' in the Japanese office for nearly three months now.

Dudley Gotla has gone up-river with a party of 300, it is said to Prangkassi.

12 June 1944

The camp population, now down to about 2,500, has been reorganised in four battalions – two British, one Dutch and one officers' (British and Dutch). There is already friction in the officers' battalion, since Colonel Swinton, who is in charge, issued 'orders' that they should all work in the camp garden, which does not, so far as I can gather, contribute to our food supplies. It was alleged that this was a Japanese order but it appears that the Japanese have admitted, rather late in the day, that they are not entitled, under the Geneva Convention, to demand that officers shall work. This is not to say that it is not a good thing for officers to work – it is of course. And that no doubt is the primary reason why Colonel Swinton, with the support of our camp HQ, has 'ordered' it. But this order has resulted in the drastic reduction of the number of officers working (and working hard) in the hospital. It is true we have not nearly so many sick men now, but we still can do with a *lot* of outside assistance – carrying water, boiling water, disinfecting clothes, doing repairs and so on. Further, the anti-malarial party, which even inside the camp area – it is not allowed by the Japs outside – is doing useful work, has been swept away. These two repercussions, on the hospital helpers and the anti-malarial party, show the lack of consideration with which our own people act. However, Major W———, as before, is leading a strong agitation against the carrying out of the order.

13 June 1944

It appears now that though the Japs did 'suggest' that more officers should work in the camp garden, they issued no orders: so that we in the hospital have to thank our own administration for the drastic cutting down in the number of our officer helpers. The anti-malarial party has been restored, however.

17 June 1944

A number of sick men from the Japan parties left behind at Non Pladuk have come back here. Some are pretty ill.

Sergeant-Major Eda of the Jap medical office has come back from Saigon. He has active amoebic dysentery – the third of the senior Jap NCOs to get it.

19 June 1944

A small party of 20 sick men, from the 'Burma' camp to which Major Read went, arrived today after a four or five day journey – fever-ridden, pale, haggard and exhausted. Tony Cator, now very thin, was in charge. At their Burma camp the food was very poor: rice plus quite inadequate quantities of dried fish, dried meat and dried vegetable. Eggs hardly obtainable. They have had a great deal of malaria.

22 June 1944

We have done blood films of all Tony Cator's party – practically 100 per cent sub-tertian malaria infections.

The party on its way down saw some signs of bombing of the railway but there was no break in the line.

26 June 1944

'Dr' Nobusawa, back from Singapore whither he went with the Japan parties, says these parties have left Singapore for 'another country'.

Our letters, which have now been in the Jap office in this camp for over three months, are still largely unissued, as Adachi will not pass out more than between ten and twenty a day: there are thousands to be done.

The camp theatre put on Emlyn Williams's *Night Must Fall* two nights ago. It was extremely well done, the tension being excellently maintained. Milsum, Ginger de Wardener and Freddie Thompson took the three chief parts and were very good indeed.

6 July 1944

A day or two ago quite large supplies of Red Cross drugs were handed out – a pleasant surprise. One of the most valuable items is 480 grains of emetine. We have an unnecessarily vast supply of calomel and cascara – drugs for which there is only too little need under these conditions. There is also a lot of anti-diphtheria serum – we could have done with it at the end of 1942. Now there is hardly any diphtheria.

Colonel Yanagida made a speech to the officers yesterday in which he said that he had been very pleased eighteen months ago when they 'agreed to help' with the railway (ironic, when one remembers their method of securing 'agree-ment') and was glad that they were now voluntarily helping in the garden.

I have been having a dengue-like fever, not bad, but depressing for a few days. The weather has been pretty wet.

The hospital lab has been built over in the Japanese area of the camp. Ian and I do the microscope work, Williams (a soils chemist from Guthrie and Company, Malaya), Jones (of the Signals) and de Fluiter (a very nice Dutch entomologist from Malang) act as technical assistants.

23 July 1944

I have had quite a severe spell of fever, apparently not malaria, for Ian did a blood slide each day for the first week and it was consistently negative, though I took no quinine of course. My temperature went up to 104 degrees each day for eight days: in each of the first three days it touched 105 degrees and I had a 'rigor'. Then it gradually fizzled out. I became extraordinarily feeble, but am picking up again. I never reached a stage when I could not get to the latrine myself, so I do not think it could have been scrub typhus.

There was a nearly total eclipse of the sun during the time I was ill. It became quite dark and gloomy. At the height of the eclipse, the sunlight coming through the pin-holes in the attap roof threw innumerable little crescents on the hut floors; by watching these images I was able to observe the course of the eclipse.

My temperature lasted from 9 to 20 July. In the middle, I received some letters – all sent off in the middle of 1943, after notification of my being a prisoner had got through. Being ill under these conditions is uncomfortable, with nothing but a ragged khaki shirt and shorts to wear, and no change of bedclothes possible in spite of all the furious sweating that I was doing; but very many men had far worse and longer illnesses, so I should not complain.

The Japs had another parade of all our sick while I was ill. They did not, one must record, make any complaints that men being marked sick were not really sick. But they said that they wanted as many men as possible marked fit so that they would get more food and become fitter.[1]

28 July 1944

The biggest floods seen here are in progress at the moment. The water has come right over the country at the back of the camp, and up to and into the lower ends of the huts in the main rows. The River Kwai Noi has also risen higher and is pouring over the bank into the cookhouses and the canteen building, and the theatre area. There has not been a great deal of rain here, but evidently there has been a lot up in the hills.

Our numbers are to be increased by one or two thousand men from 3 Group who are at Tamarkan and beginning to arrive here in small parties. They are Australians and Dutch, and a few Americans. They have come to Siam by way of Burma, having been taken to the far end of our railway from Singapore by boat in May 1942. They have had a bad time at intervals of greater or less length – bad food and brutal treatment. Four of their men are said to have been shot for talking with Burmese against Jap orders.

I am still rather feeble from my fever, but improving, and appetite good again.

8 August 1944

A Japanese private soldier, said to have been knifed by another in a pot-house brawl in Kanburi, has died. The Japanese have just given him a funeral. A basket-ball match, and a concert which had been arranged in our camp, were forbidden by the Japs on account of the ceremony. There is a striking contrast between this elaborate observance and the complete indifference of the Japanese to our deaths – *they* didn't even stop playing tennis in the camp in the bad days when 15 or 16 bodies a day were being carried to the cemetery from our hospital, past their rough earth tennis court.

Three more letters yesterday, two from Mother, one from Margaret Cameron.

18 August 1944

Charles Fisher told me today a good story of Alfred Webb's about Colonel J――――― of an Indian regiment. Alfred (a chaplain) was walking round the cemetery and met J and they were looking at the graves when J noticed the column bearing a star which marked a Jewish grave. 'What is that?' asked the colonel. Alfred told him. 'Ah,' he nodded. 'I suppose that is the Star of Bethlehem?' Alfred protested, saying no, the Jews are not Christians. 'Oh,'

[1] Note by RSH. Their system was to issue a smaller ration for people who were sick. They arrived at the total camp ration issue by multiplying the total number fit by the full ration, and the total number of sick by the 'reduced' ration quantities, and adding the two. They almost appear to have believed that we then took care to see that the actual sick got reduced rations. Of course we never did this.

said J. 'Not Christians? Really?' It was Colonel J who, at Wang Lan, while acting as 'storeman' on a pile of stores beside the line, was hailed by an irate Japanese some distance off, who yelled 'Wi-ah! 'Wi-ah!' Colonel J saw he wanted something and held up a spade interrogatively. The Jap yelled more furiously. J held up something else, vaguely. A colleague said to him hurriedly, 'I think he wants wire.' 'Oh,' said the colonel, 'Wah? If he wants wah, why doesn't he say "Wah"?' It was also Colonel J, Charles says, who made the great remark about a fellow officer who had the first and second fingers of his right hand shot away, 'Ah well, it won't affect him – he doesn't shoot.' I remembered the Punch joke of the two old colonels meeting at Bisley in 1919, 'Nice to be back at Bisley again – hasn't been any serious shooting since 1913'; and also a quite serious remark I heard not long ago from an Indian Army major, 'Oh to be back in India again, where one can do one's soldiering under proper conditions.'

20 August 1944

There is a rumour that all the sick in this camp are to be moved over to Tamarkan, leaving only fit men in this camp to look after the garden.

Small parties of sick arrive here from time to time from up-river. Yesterday 30 men came in from Hindato – all anaemic malarial wrecks, six very sick indeed. Of 18 slides from them examined today, 16 were positive sub-tertian, many with numerous crescents. Six days ago they got some quinine, which we had sent up from here on receiving an SOS from them. Previous to that for quite a long time they had none at all. Their food had been shocking but improved a lot when Lieutenant Noguchi (the bearded officer) went up from here. In comparison we are living in luxury, with the canteen producing excellent, cheap, supplementary meals.

27 August 1944

Another flood outside; but an earth bank, which was incomplete when the last rise of the rivers took place, had been completed this time and the water did not seriously invade the camp. Clarke has gone up to Konkuita with a party of 100, and Renes is about to go up to Hindato with 250 Dutch.

Yesterday the Nip medical authorities ordered a parade of all our sick. 'Dr' Nobusawa and Sergeant-Major Eda were present, but Nobusawa merely sat and watched while Eda decided which of the sick should work and which not. Eda decided that out of a total of nearly 400 only 37 were seriously ill. The rest could be considered 'light sick', as the Jap term is. Of the 213 'light sick' who had malaria, Eda decided that 200 should work. The Japs say that the 'Nippon Number One' is coming, so the medical authorities are evidently getting ready to show him favourable figures. A curious commentary is the attitude of the Jap administrative side; they will not accept for work the men Eda marked yesterday as fit, for they know they are not fit and they are having a feud with their medical side.

I had a renal colic some days ago – a painful, but fortunately brief, experience.

I think I have recovered all the weight I lost in my fever of July. I am feeling pretty well now.

I have been reading Lin Yu Tang's *Moment in Pekin*, a brilliant picture of Chinese life in the first three or four decades of this century. My light camp-bed mattress, which has only survived so long in consequence of the anxious care I have taken of it in sewing and darning the rents which have kept developing, has finally had to be scrapped, since the hut cat in my absence started to have kittens on it. I have made a half-length substitute using the cloth of my old valise, stuffed with the kapok from the old mattress.

I have just obtained from our office the figures for *deaths* in POW camps in Siam up to three or four months ago.

Original Group	British	Australian	Dutch	Total
Saigon	31 (out of 388)			31/388
1	156 (out of 2071)	216 (out of 370)	1167 (out of 5374)	1539/7815
2	1114 (out of 5650)		265 (out of 1620)	1379/7270
3	128 (out of 367)	725 (out of 4138)	931 (out of 4847)	1784/9352
4	1700 (out of 7257)	390 (out of 2511)	115 (out of 1678)	2245/11446
Kanburi	405 (out of 4745)	18 (out of 153)	98 (out of 994)	521/5892
Totals % of Total Population	3534 15.2%	1349 15.2%	2616 15.0%	7499/42163

In addition, one must reckon on nearly 6,000 out of the 10,000 in the Nikki parties being dead. This makes a total of over 13,400 dead.

5 September 1944

The fifth year of war ended two days ago, and that night we heard again the hum of aero-engines and the faint rumble of bombs somewhere. Hope is strong that this sixth year of war will bring our captivity to an end.

Rumours are increasing that all the sick in this camp are to move to Tamarkan and that, with the exception of a party to look after the garden, all the fit will be going up the line again to do repairs.

This camp was recently 'inspected' by the new Colonel Superintendent of POW Camps, but no one saw him. Colonel Yanagida subsequently 'transmitted' his message to look after our healths, to look forward to repatriation, and to keep our discipline for the honour of our country; and not to try to escape.

It is said that leaflets have been found along the river, obviously dropped by aeroplanes; they are said to claim that the war in Europe is going well for us. One is reported to have in large letters a final exhortation, 'Hold on! We are coming.' This fills us with hope.

I have had one or two more letters – written in the early part of 1943, before the notification of prisoners' names.

Hajji Marsh has made me a really comfortable bed out of bamboo and an old piece of canvas. I am able to sleep really well again.

11 September 1944

On the night of 6 September aeroplanes were over and we heard bombs. And we have learned that the railway at Non Pladuk was bombed, with about 80 Dutch and British killed and 200 wounded.[1] A Japanese camp is said also to have been hit, and a fair amount of damage done to the railway track, sidings and trucks. The majority of the killed and wounded were Dutch, who had very unluckily just that day arrived at Non Pladuk and had been temporarily accommodated in a hut outside the POW camp and near the line. Leaflets were found afterwards, of an encouraging nature, we gather.

Walker is standing by to go up-river with another party. These parties get very little quinine from the Nips here to take with them and when they get up there are kept extremely short – all the sick coming down have had totally inadequate amounts.

Since the Colonel Superintendent's visit we have been having morning and evening roll-calls again. The absent (sick in lines, cooks on duty and so on) constitute quite a large number, but they are counted, so it is hard to see the value of the roll-call. Our rations have deteriorated, as the number of sick men in this camp has increased. There has been a qualitative deterioration as well as quantitative.

There is also a shortage of firewood as the Nips issue insufficient for all the cooking we do, and the available bamboo and trees in the camp are exhausted. No firewood parties are now allowed out of the camp. The hospital, which needs a lot of fuel for boiling water, disinfecting clothes, distilling spirit and water, and sterilising utensils, is in great difficulties. And the canteen's style is also cramped.

Ian and I are digging some ground to plant tomatoes near our hut; I have a small bed of kankong (creeping spinach) as well.

25 September 1944

A party of 600 to go up-river has been called for by the Japanese. We simply haven't got so many fit men. Of the best 600, at least 200 are unfit, and we are hoping to persuade Nobusawa to look at them. Colonel T[2] at Tamarkan is said to have told the Japs there firmly that he had no further fit men, and that they would have to assume full responsibility; with the result that they are trying to take the men from this camp.

4 October 1944

Benson, Metz and MacArthur have all gone up-river again with working parties. It was extremely difficult to find the number of men for the last party

[1] The final casualty toll was 100 dead and 400 wounded.
[2] Lieutenant-Colonel P J D (later Brigadier Sir Philip) Toosey, Royal Artillery, one of the outstanding camp commandants on the railway.

and even Nobusawa, who was appealed to, admitted that the men were not fit to go; but, he said, they must go, for so it had been ordered by a higher authority (on the strength of his misrepresentations earlier of the number of sick?). He said they could be sent down again very soon. This actually happened at Kinsaiyok, I think. A party that had just been sent up was sent down again by the Kinsaiyok camp commander the next day because they were obviously useless for work.

I am reading an interesting book of Charles Fisher's, the diary of Erwin Bälz, a German physiologist who went to Japan in 1875. He writes good, simple, lucid German, and is very interesting on the Japanese as he saw them.

15 October 1944

Parties from Burma coming down to this camp have greatly increased the number of sick in the hospital. My malaria ward, which I started two weeks ago with 80 men or so, now has over 200, some very anaemic. Japanese quinine issues are now quite inadequate and we are having to be more sparing in treatment than we should like.[1]

Colonel Williamson and the rest of our camp HQ have today gone off to Tamarkan.

A Dutch party recently down from the Burma border reports that when their supplies of American Red Cross drugs came some months ago the Japanese issued them; but next day demanded back all the atebrin and all the M & B 693, and each Japanese soldier in the camp was given one tin of M & B (500 tablets) and one bottle of atebrin (200 tablets). The Japanese commandant himself took the lint, which he made into three pairs of pyjamas and a set of curtains for his hut.

18 October 1944

Colonel Owtram, Innes and others were unceremoniously turned out of their hut near ours at half an hour's notice today. We feel our hut is likely to be the next to go. Colonel Owtram's was wanted by the Nips as a recreation hut for the Koreans.

Charles Fisher has been at Tamarkan for a day or two. He says their feeding is much better than ours, but the camp and quarters much more cramped.

31 October 1944

Four days ago a party of 200 was suddenly formed to go up-country – some fit, but a large number chronic malarias. Ian was attached to it as medical officer. They left at midnight on 26 October. Charles Mounsey was one of the officers in the party, and Clarkson and Woodward were taken from the canteen, which they have been running very well, to go with it. They have only been up-river for a very short time (in 1943) and are both fit; they recognise that it is better for fit men like them to go up again rather than unfit men who have perhaps already been up for longer. We don't know yet where Ian's party has gone to.

[1] Note by RSH. We had a reserve which Ian Mackintosh had accumulated from somewhere which was extremely useful, in fact vital.

Bombers were overhead three nights ago, perhaps on a visit to Bangkok or Non Pladuk.

A chatty Korean says that Colonel Yanagida told them that 250,000 Americans recently landed on the Philippines, but have all been taken prisoner.

Here are four Japanese propaganda stories which have appeared in either the *Nippon Times* (a paper published in Japan, in English) or the local Siamese papers.

1. An account is given of how one of the Japanese 'War Eagles' (fighter pilots) finding himself run out of ammunition when attacking American bombers, in desperation seized his 'rice-cake' (presumably his lunch) and hurled it at an enemy bomber; it hit its mark and the bomber fell out of control.

2. Another War Eagle, out of ammunition in an attack on American ships in the Solomons, swooped on the bridge of a cruiser, drew his sword and, as he whizzed by, sliced off the American commander's head.

3. A pilot coming in to land found that his undercarriage had been shot away. Opening the throttle and pulling out into a circuit of the aerodrome to consider the situation, he had an idea. He hastily cut two holes in the floor of his cockpit with a knife. As he came in to land, he dropped his legs through these holes and, running desperately, ultimately brought his machine to a stop.

4. A Second Class Japanese private has been specially decorated in the Pacific for carrying an important message from one island to another by swimming. The message was 'too secret and important to be sent by radio', so it was entrusted to a 'surer means', and was delivered by the swimmer after he had been in the water for forty-eight hours.

14 November 1944

It has become clear that the Japanese plan at present is to take us all over to Tamarkan within a fairly short period, leaving only a small party here to look after the garden. A colonel or general of the Nip army has paid a visit to this camp – he walked rapidly round it, not looking at anything in the prisoners' area longer than a glance. As a result, Nobusawa tells us, he has severely criticised the work of the British and Dutch medical officers in this camp; they are not striving to improve the men's health. At the same time, far too many men who are fit to work are being shown as sick!

Pending an evacuation, the camp is to be drastically reduced in size.

Nobusawa yesterday came over to the hospital to decide which of the patients should be allowed to remain in hospital, and which were fit for work. As usual he paid no attention to our representations. He decided that a number of men in their third and fourth day of malaria were fit to go up-river to work. All the convalescent amoebics, whom we have kept living apart, were turned out of hospital and the Japs actually insisted on their all going up-country the next day. Altogether Nobusawa turned nearly fifty per cent of the men out of hospital.

Over at Tamarkan the Jap general had Colonel Williamson and Colonel Hamilton (Australian Army Medical Corps) summoned and asked them through an interpreter for frank suggestions as to the welfare of the prisoners. Colonel Hamilton, who had all the points ready, began with the huts. He was going to say that in the first place the overcrowding made cleanliness and health impossible; but he was interrupted. The general simply said that now that the weather was better, better huts were not necessary. He then turned to Colonel Williamson, who asked for an assurance that sick men would not be sent up-country to work. 'That is impossible,' replied the general and the interview was abruptly closed.

15 November 1944

Today the Japanese have demanded that all officers helping in the hospital (about 70) should be withdrawn to work in the camp. There are nearly 500 men in hospital, none of them (after all the inspections Nobusawa has made to throw out those 'fit for work') able to do much to help themselves. We have about 60 orderlies, but they have to man the cookhouse, carry meals and water and attend to all the nursing, such as it is, and 70 extra helpers are none too many. The Japs simply haven't any idea of the numbers necessary to keep things going under these primitive conditions. They say that at the big hospital camp of Nakom Paton there are only 19 orderlies per 1,000 patients; but they lose sight of the fact that in that camp very great numbers of convalescent patients are employed about the hospital, for as that is a definite hospital camp they do not suffer 'blitzes' to find labour to work on the railway.

21 November 1944

The hospital here, it appears, is to be closed. The 200 sickest are to go to Tamarkan – 100 are actually to leave today, mostly malarias with anaemia – and the remainder are, one supposes, to be reabsorbed in their battalions, sick as they are. But even if the two hundred worst cases are taken away, there will be plenty more very sick men with the malaria incidence as it is at present, and there will have to be some arrangements to cope with them. A great many very sick men are coming down to Tamarkan from up-river just now – Tamajo, beyond Takanun, is having a very bad time with sub-tertian malaria, a lot of it cerebral. Tamarkan must have a very large number of sick men now.

My tomatoes have begun to ripen. I have made some remarkably good chutney with the deformed ones, using sugar, ginger, onions and vinegar.

28 November 1944

The amoebic dysentery cases from the hospital went over to Tamarkan this morning. Another party of 250 (the Japanese have not, in the end, limited the transfer to the 200 sickest men) is to go tomorrow. There are about 1,400 people in this camp now.

We hear that 20 men have died at Tamajo of sub-tertian malaria, and others, desperately ill, have come down to Tamarkan.

Two days ago we heard the siren alarms go in Kanburi and heard some extremely distant explosions, but saw no planes.

30 November 1944

Yesterday evening, in the last rays of the setting sun, 21 big four-engined bombers came in low over Tamarkan, passing to the north of this camp, and dropped some bombs in the region of the bridge, which is three or four miles away from here. The anti-aircraft guns fired for a little without effect. Last night we heard one or two trains going up, so we infer that the bridge has not been broken. Today we have heard that some of the bombs fell in the POW camp; 14 men were killed and 30 injured.[1]

One wonders if this bombing of the Tamarkan area will affect the decision to transfer all our sick from here. Yesterday, just before the raid, Duncan Black and 50 officers were transferred over to Tamarkan.

7 December 1944

A day or two after the bombing of Tamarkan where, apparently, little damage was done except to POWs, we saw another (or perhaps the same) force of 21 bombers going back north westwards after the siren at Kanburi had blown, and we had heard the rumble of a big cargo of bombs from the Non Pladuk direction.

We have been digging slit trenches here along the sides of the huts. And the Nips have been digging little round holes in the ground in their area.

Yesterday another 60 sick men went down to Tamarkan.

9 December 1944

A party of 200 (half-day workers!) with Alec Dunlop and half a dozen 'anti-malarial officers' has been formed to go up-river soon. These men are not fit to go up-river to work but we can't prevent it.

Last night about 6.45pm, when I was playing baseball on the open recreation area, we heard the siren at Kanburi and all trooped off to the neighbourhood of our slit trenches. After nearly half an hour's waiting, a big four-engined bomber passed directly overhead, going east; when it was over the Kanburi area we saw three bombs fall. Two more bombers followed, and dropped their bombs at the same point. One of these machines turned towards Tamarkan and fired machine guns or cannon at the anti-aircraft guns, which had been shooting ineffectively while the planes made their runs over Kanburi. Some more runs were made and we could see smoke rising in the distance. When the all-clear came half an hour later it was quite dark and we could see a red glow in the sky in the direction of Kanburi.

The earliness of the warning before the arrival of the planes over Kanburi suggests that they had attacked other objectives earlier, and in fact a faint red glow was observed in the sky to the north-west after it got dark.

From our slit trenches we had a fine view of the big bombers (Liberators) cruising around.

A steam train and a diesel train went up the railway during the night, so the bridge is still all right.

15 December 1944

There has been a good deal of aerial activity in these last few days.

Two nights ago there was more bombing over Kanburi, with a great

[1] The official figures are 18 POWs killed and 68 wounded.

amount of fruitless shooting by the Tamarkan anti-aircraft guns.

Yesterday morning the hum and throb of numbers of planes was heard for quite a long time during the morning, and there were distant explosions which seemed to come from the Non Pladuk area; there was a lot of low broken cloud and we did not see the bombers. Then, yesterday evening just before sunset, in fine weather, a really heavy attack was made on the Kanburi HQ camp area. About 15 bombers seemed to be engaged – all Liberators – and each made several runs over the target. Many flew directly over this camp on their way in to bomb, and from our slit trenches we had an excellent view as they flew east over to Kanburi and released their bombs. There were heavy explosions, and as dusk fell the glare of incendiaries and great mounting clouds of black smoke lit by red flashes made a fine picture over the trees to the east. The anti-aircraft guns at Tamarkan did a lot of shooting, but without any obvious result. The guns are too far away (about four miles, I suppose) to be able to shoot at planes over Kanburi; they could only take shots at the bombers if they passed near on their way in to the target or coming away from it.

We have heard some distant explosions up the line, too, so the railway further up has probably been attacked. It is not likely that it has been broken since Alec Dunlop's party, which was to have gone to Tamajo and was put off, has been warned to be ready to leave tonight. There has been some light diesel traffic on the railway and we know that the bridge at Tamarkan is working still – it has not in fact been seriously attacked, beyond a little shooting up with machine guns and cannon.

18 December 1944

As a result of the air attacks in this neighbourhood, the Japanese decision to transfer all but a small number of personnel from this camp to Tamarkan has apparently been reversed, and the Tamarkan personnel, at least the sick, are being transferred here. Apparently morale at Tamarkan among the prisoners has been much shaken by the original attack, in which some POWs were killed, and by the more recent machine-gunning which has been going on during raids – although since the original bomb casualties no one has been injured. But there has been great competition among officers and men there to get back to this camp, which is far enough away from the bridge and from Kanburi to give one a feeling of complete security during raids, but near enough to give one excellent views of the bombers as they go round.

There has evidently been a bit of bombing up the line. People who have come over from Tamarkan report that about 40 wounded men came down there the other day from Prangkassi and Wang Yai. Many were stretcher cases: they took eight days to do the 150 kilometres. They spent most of the time on sidings, the Japs evidently making little attempt to pass them down quickly. At Kinsaiyok the guards have become very violent since the bombing began. Men in their second and third day of malaria have been compelled to work. A lot of them are collapsing and some parties of completely exhausted wrecks are coming down to Tamarkan from there.

Nearly 1,000 men have come over from Tamarkan; many men who are really unfit to walk the distance have made the attempt, so unnerved is the camp over there by the raids. An officer is actually said to have offered a cheque for £100 to another officer to take his place on a party coming over here.

While the big raid on Kanburi was beginning the other night, Kokuba, the Jap local camp commandant, seeing people running for slit trenches, charged excitedly out of his office waving his drawn sword and shouting, so the interpreter Punt says, 'Keep calm! Keep calm! Or I will kill you!'

27 December 1944

Another Christmas has come and gone. The Japanese made a special issue of extra meat and fruit. This is probably not spontaneous generosity, for we think that they are holding quite a sum of Red Cross money though they will not explicitly say so. But our people working in the HQ office have picked up hints which suggest it.

Consequently our food this Christmas was better than usual and the customary effort was made, with extra subscriptions, to have a really good spread all round. The results were excellent. A pantomime Cinderella was put on by the theatre people, which was a great success.

The only discordant note on Christmas Day was provided by Kokuba, the Jap commandant, who, obviously under the influence of liquor, took a walk round the camp in the afternoon with a fellow officer. He unfortunately found a gap in an internal fence near a Dutch hut, and a perfectly innocent Dutchman, who happened to be near at hand, got a very severe beating up. Although

Chungkai, 21 December 1944

of course he had nothing to do with making the gap, Kokuba knocked him about quite savagely, drunk as he was. During the proceedings he frequently turned round to his fellow officer, grinning horribly, as if to say, 'That's the way to treat these dogs.'

I wonder if this is the last Christmas we shall spend in captivity?

Pat MacArthur, Benson and Adams are back in Tamarkan from up-river with their parties. Clarkson, down to get canteen goods for Ian's camp, reports that conditions up there are not at all bad. But Charles Fisher, back today from Kinsaiyok, reports that rations up-river are deteriorating, since, in view of air raids, trains now only run during the night.

1 January 1945

The New Year opens quietly. There have been plenty of air raid warnings recently (by the camp field telephone and by the Kanburi siren) but we have seen and heard nothing here. The raids are presumably on other parts of Siam or the railway line elsewhere.

Nearly two thousand men have now come over to this camp from Tamarkan. A great many of them have malaria – there has been a very serious shortage at Tamarkan of quinine, and no plasmoquine. Our position here, with this great influx of men with fever, is pretty desperate too. The Japanese say they are very short of quinine and are having difficulty in getting it. One has heard this story before, put forward to cover mere indifference – but of course it might be true. A great number of the malarias coming in from Tamarkan are sub-tertians.

In the first half of December, before the Tamarkan people came over, we had altogether 16 positive sub-tertians, 216 positive benign tertians and 9 double infections in this camp. In the second half of the month we had 178 positive sub-tertians, 402 benign tertians and 117 double infections. Thus, as well as a great increase in the *total* number, there is a great increase in the *proportion* of sub-tertians to benign tertians – about five times as many sub-tertians in a given number of malarias.

9 January 1945

Two more postcards (25 words) and three letters – one of them dating from 1943. The others belong to March–May 1944. These are really quite recent!

Colonel Ishii and his No. 2 Group HQ staff have transferred over here from Tamarkan, and the conditions of life have at once become more irksome because all the tinpot Jap authorities feel they must be extra officious under the colonel's eye.

The worst feature by far of the present state of affairs is that the half-day workers are usually being worked about 18 hours a day. They do their four hours in the morning. But in the afternoon, say, a barge comes in with rice or something of that sort – the Jap office at once calls out the half-day workers. Then some Jap decides that the rebuilding of the huts or the carrying of bamboo or attap or the construction of Jap shelters or fences is not going on fast enough, so the half-day workers are called out again in the evening and may be kept working all night.

Or an extra effort is asked, with a promise of a holiday the next day. The effort is made, but next day no one on the Jap side remembers about the holiday.

Other minor irritations are (i) The restriction of the bathing area and the limitation of the periods during which one may bathe in the river. (ii) The calling in by the Japanese for censoring of all the books in the camps – these books have been read and reread, and passed around for nearly three years without censoring – and the announcement, when that had been done, that the stamp for marking them as approved had not been brought over from Tamarkan, so we must wait, entirely bookless meanwhile. The Japanese added that there were in any case a lot of letters still to censor, and these would have preference over the books. (iii) There is to be only one theatrical performance a week. The theatre only holds at most a third of the camp.

The sick returns have now to be much more elaborate than they used to be, and their preparation takes a lot of time. Each unit has to hand in a nominal roll of its sick, stating in each case the number of days each man has been off work. And the dispensary has to report daily the amounts of drugs issued by tablets, or by weight or volume.

Needless to say, by neither of these new rules do the Japanese get to know what we don't want them to know. Our techniques for protecting the sick, by manipulation of figures, and our faking of the drug returns to conceal illicit stocks and their consumption, are quite surprisingly elaborate.

The 'Nippon Number One' – the dog-faced general – is said to be coming to this camp to inspect it today.

11 January 1945

The dog-faced general's inspection was the usual smart walk down the central roadway, out at the camp gate and round by the camp boundary to the north where work is going on at present on the big ditch which is being dug right round the camp. Hardly a glance at the huts, and no inspection at all of the occupants or of the hospital.

'Andy' (Lieutenant Anderson) the dispenser, notified Sergeant-Major Eda today that our quinine was finished. He replied lazily that he would write to HQ. We've been agitating for months for better supplies: he hasn't even taken the trouble yet to find out whether he can get more. The incidence of sub-tertian infections is still rising.

15 January 1945

The sending of the sick out to work continues. Nobusawa sees and chooses them himself as we of course are not 'reliable'. The other day, after choosing 80 ill-looking men from a party newly arrived in the camp, he met our protests with, 'Do not worry. I have examined them and they will not die.' Two days ago the Nips ordered the sick and light duty workers to move 3,100 sacks of rice, dumped beside the railway a quarter of a mile outside the camp, into one of the store huts. Our HQ protested, but the order would have been enforced had it not been decided that the fit men in the camp would do the job in their free time. So we all trooped out and carried these heavy sacks. The rice sacks were about 50 kilograms – 112lb – and one had to carry them about 500 yards. I carried three and shared a bag of soya beans (200lb) with another labourer. It was really hard work, quite beyond the capacity of sick men.

Ian's party arrived back this morning after a three-day journey. Ian and other friends in the party are well – Mounsey, Clarkson, Woodward. They have not had a bad time at Kurikonta, but felt they had got down just in time, as these far up-river camps have been very much out of touch, with the damage recently done to the railway. It was evidently sufficiently patched, however, to bring them down. At the time of the bombing attacks up-river there was a period of ten days when no train passed in either direction.

Last night, waiting in a siding, they heard the aircraft which we heard here, but they passed on to Bangkok and did not touch the railway.

Nobusawa disgorged a 5-kilo tin of quinine powder today – it must last a fortnight, he said.

Sick parties are still coming across from Tamarkan, some of them collapsing en route. They are made to walk unless obviously bedridden, but the distance (three or four miles) is far too much for many of them. Quite a number usually collapse on the railway track, along which they struggle, and have to be carried in. If we treated the sub-tertian malarias alone properly, the 5 kilos of quinine would not last five days. With our hidden reserves we can at present afford five days' treatment at 1.0gm daily for sub-tertians, and three for the bad benign tertians. The Nips still will not allow any extension of the hospital accommodation although it is desperately needed. With malarias in hospital and the lab I have been pretty busy but In't Veld (a Dutch doctor – very competent indeed) has been helping a lot, and now that Ian is back the lab will be less arduous. De Fluiter – the Dutch entomologist who acts as technical assistant and is of course fully competent to examine slides – has been a tower of strength.

19 January 1945

Nobusawa continues to hold parades of the sick men coming over from Tamarkan, and sends out to work men with severe anaemias, tachycardia and other conditions in spite of protests. We manage usually to swap the worst of them afterwards for less decrepit individuals and so prevent his decisions from doing too much harm. Nobusawa continues to refuse further hospital accommodation; we can still not accommodate more than 120 or so, and that only with intense crowding. The Junyi (Japanese RSM) has told us that a new hut for the dispensary, laboratory, operating room and for the medical officers' quarters is to be put up in the area at present occupied by the officers' gardens alongside the cemetery. If we can retain the hut accommodation where we now are, for the hospital, we may be able to find room for more patients.

26 January 1945

Nobusawa continues to hold his sick parades over in the Jap area, giving the sick a distance of several hundred yards to walk, instead of himself coming over to see them. One of the men whom he pronounced to be fit for work had so low a haemoglobin that it had already been decided that he should have a blood transfusion. The big ditch round the camp (10 feet deep and 15 feet wide) is being pushed on as rapidly as possible – apparently the dog-faced general is very keen on getting it completed – and it is for this heavy work that all the workers are demanded.

It is clear that there is fresh malaria occurring in this camp area, no doubt as a result of the abandonment of the anti-malarial precautions outside the camp, which were so effective before. Robin Calderwood, who has not previously had malaria, is down with sub or benign tertian, and there are many other similar cases. But of course it is difficult to know how much malaria is fresh, not relapse, since about 95 per cent of the camp have had malaria fairly recently.

Stories coming down from Wampo, where a lot of prisoners are working strung out on the hill track towards Tavoy repairing the track and carrying rice to dumps along the road, show that conditions there are much what they were in 1943 : sleeping in the open, rations rice and dried veg alone. Men working all the time while sick, and only sent down here as sick when they are so ill that even a Nipponese can see that they are going to be no use for months, even if they don't die. Hatreed brought 100 down the other day.

We have at present 1,250 or so men in camp not working on account of malaria, and today Nobusawa gave orders that a numbered blood smear on a glass slide was to be made for each of these, even though they are under treatment. A list of names, giving the number of the slide, had to be prepared, in a hurry as usual. A phenomenal number will be positive if the examination is competently done, for few benign tertians get any quinine, and sub-tertians, we know, are often positive two or three days after treatment has begun. To make sure that the majority of the slides were positive we faked them. We got hold of several men in the acute early stage of fever, rapidly tested their blood to make sure it was positive and smeared it on the great majority of the 1,250 slides : so we shall know how accurate the Japanese microscopists are.

31 January 1945

Nobusawa told Max Pemberton today, with an air of triumph, that of the 1,264 slides we sent in only 135 showed sub-tertian, 191 benign tertian and four double infections – in other words 25 per cent. If he knew his job he would think that this was about right since one might suspect about three-quarters of those under treatment to be negative. But in fact this result only shows that the microscopists did not make a proper examination, for we *know* that about 90 per cent of the slides must have been positive, because we were careful to make them so. We heard later from Squadron Leader Cumming – a medical officer, RAF, who worked for a time in the Jap laboratory at Kanburi – that proper examinations of blood films were *not* made in the Jap laboratory. They took a few random samples and filled up the bulk of the returns without microscopic examination at all. Nobusawa evidently thinks that the 25 per cent positive result sent up by the Jap lab proves that we are greatly inflating our malaria returns. For once we are not doing so, for whatever returns we put in we get so little quinine from the Japs that it is not worth while inflating them.

The theatre is to be pulled down tomorrow – the interpreter is said to have stated that it is not right that we should enjoy ourselves when the Japanese in Burma and Japan are being bombed.

158

Nobusawa is working through the whole of the camp sick – two battalions a day – to make sure that no fit men are not working. He selected a number from Nos. 4 and 5 Battalions yesterday for half-day work. The half-day workers did three or four hours in the morning and were all called out again at 11pm to work on the big ditch at night. The Japs say it must be finished today. Perhaps the dog-faced general is in the vicinity again.

HQ have been notified by the Nips that all officers, except medical officers, will shortly be leaving this camp, apparently to go to the camp at Kanburi. Warrant officers will be left to run the camp here.

A big party of 3,000 is to go to Ratburi or Petchaburi to build an aerodrome. Seven hundred are to go from this camp: all the medical officers at present at Tamarkan are to go – Commander Epstein, United States Navy; Major Black, Indian Medical Service; Major Read, Royal Army Medical Corps; Sykes; Gotla; de Wardener; Walker; two Australian medical officers and a dentist.

The position as regards money for the hospital will be very difficult when the officers go. It is true that such contributions have for some time been banned by the Japs, with a vague promise of subventions from them (we think they are holding some Red Cross Funds) but of course they have been maintained, though not openly.[1] The hospital will have difficulty in replacing its voluntary officer helpers and perhaps in maintaining the dietetic supplements which are so beneficial at present.

The ditch and fence round the camp have been completed. This ditch also separates us from the river, access to which is much restricted.

Yesterday a Japanese official photographer visited the camp. All fit men were specially paraded and taken to the bathing place on the river, where the rules about bathing – not going in beyond a certain distance – were temporarily suspended. Everyone was instructed to 'look happy' and the Jap took some pictures, no doubt for propaganda.

Squadron Leader Taylor, who has done extremely good work in the hospital cookhouse organising special diets for more than a year, will be going with the other officers. He will be hard to replace.

2 February 1945

At their sick parade camp 'bed-downs' today Nobusawa and Eda instituted two new categories, one-hour workers and two-hour workers. One fears that once these men are out they will be kept out – as the half-day workers were today. They had to parade at 6am and worked all morning. In the afternoon they were called out again and kept out for three hours.

The Japanese are now actually issuing two eggs a day extra for every man on full-day work, as an attraction. It is an attraction to a half-day man who works a full day anyway! The half-day workers get no extra ration. Full-day workers are doing very long hours. Their reveille this morning was 4am.

The first party of officers is standing by to go to Kanburi. Andy and Jack

[1] Note by RSH. Elaborate double book-keeping by experts at the canteen – Clarkson of J. A. Russell and Co., Kuala Lumpur, was one and Woodward, a chartered accountant in civil life, another – was necessary to conceal the extensive hospital purchases with the secret funds. The cash was kept concealed – it had one or two narrow escapes during Japanese searches, which I have not recorded.

Masefield, who work in the dispensary, are the only two combatant officers who will be remaining with us.

9 February 1945

The first party of 250 officers left four days ago – on Monday, this being Friday. They went to Tamarkan. That same evening a heavy air attack was made on the bridge and the sidings near it. Two high-level runs by several aircraft opened the proceedings. Their bombs were apparently directed at the anti-aircraft defences, for when it was over there was much less anti-aircraft fire. Then the big bombers began to go in low, mostly coming down the railway line which runs quite close to this camp and flying on straight to the bridge, with cannon and machine guns going. There were some big explosions from the direction of the bridge, and we hear that the wooden bridge, which is almost a hundred yards downstream from the concrete and steel bridge, has been badly unsettled and isn't taking any traffic. After the main attack was over, a detachment of six planes made several wide circuits over the bridge and the surrounding country and dropped a number of red and white flares or bombs – some of them seemed to explode when they hit the ground. It was an impressive and inspiring sight in the fine sunny evening, though doubtless not so pleasant for the people in the bridge camp. But no prisoners sustained any injuries.

Another 150 officers are to go to Tamarkan tomorrow – but their final destination appears to be Kanburi, so they may not be at Tamarkan for long.

Nobusawa continues his reviews of the sick – they all have to make their way to *his* part of the camp, ill as they are.

The Japs have agreed to let the hospital take over some end sections in the next-door hut – enough to accommodate about 80 more men. Some very sick men from up-river and from Tamarkan are still coming in from time to time.

It appears that this camp is to contribute 1,200 men, not 700, to the new group which is to go to Ratburi, or somewhere near there, 'to build an aerodrome'. There are actually only about 800 full-day workers in this camp, in spite of Nobusawa's best efforts, so that it looks as though some unfit men will have to go. The total camp population at present is 3,890 or so, of whom 1,110 are Dutch. There are to be no Dutch in this new party. The Dutch supplied a party a few days ago to go to Ban Pong to work. Velds went with them as medical officer.

Ishii is said to have given a talk to the Korean troops here, telling them that when the British troops come they must die to a man – but they must dispose of the prisoners first!

14 February 1945

I mentioned earlier a party of a hundred 'half-day workers' sent up-river to Wampo by the Nips to work on the track from Wampo westwards towards Tavoy. We now hear from Pitt, who is up there, that they are doing exceptionally heavy full-day work. For getting their supplies along this track the Nips tried horses, then cattle; as they were unsatisfactory, prisoners are now being used as beasts of burden. Their food is bad, as often as not they are scattered in bivouacs along the track and it is only occasionally that Pitt is able to see any of them.

Yesterday evening there was another heavy raid on the bridge. The wooden bridge had by this time been repaired, and traffic was being gingerly worked over the steel bridge. The machines all dropped some heavy bombs. There was a good deal of cannon and machine-gun firing. We do not yet know what damage was done at the bridge, but at dawn today the Nips sent 150 men over from here to start repairs.

Colonel Sugasawa (the dog-faced 'general') is coming to this camp again 'on inspection' in the next day or two. Last time he merely walked quickly through the camp. But in fear lest he should look into the hospital, Nobusawa today went through it himself and insisted on discharging all the men who, he thought, 'looked too well'. Two of his choices were men with almost complete paralysis of the legs – totally unable to walk. This was pointed out to him, but he said they must go out of hospital, as they 'looked fit'.

The Japanese 'Thailand Number One Medical Officer' was here a day or two ago, also 'on inspection'. He went straight to the Japanese part of the camp, where he appears to have had a chat with Nobusawa. He then repaired to the Jap officers' quarters, and was helped out of the camp later in the evening, very drunk. He certainly came nowhere near the hospital area. The more responsible their position, apparently, the less trouble they take to find out what they are responsible for.

22 February 1945

Colonel Sugasawa visited this camp, but did not come to the prisoners' area.

Workers who have been going to Tamarkan to do repairs and to ferry material across the river pending repairs, report that the steel bridge is completely kaput and has been abandoned, two spans being dropped in the water by the last attack. Repairs are being carried out on the wooden bridge, and it is said that it will be working again before long.

All the officers have now left this camp – except the medical officers. The camp is run by warrant officers and senior NCOs. Edkins, the camp RSM, is doing extremely well.

Groups of men are leaving the camp on alterate days for the Ratburi camp. Many of them are by no means fit.

Our rations here are pretty poor at present. It is necessary to supplement the diet of people in hospital to a considerable extent; the Japanese still talk vaguely of giving us money for this purpose and some extra supplies, but nothing has materialised though we make repeated representations.

Harry Malet's diary, which he kept up at Kanyu in 1943, has come into my hands. It ends in April 1943, shortly before he died. His diary shows clearly the awful shortage of supplies – and that, when canteen supplies came in, the Japanese seized the occasion or excuse to cut down the ration issues still more. Harry kept fit until near the end, but had to work terribly hard. The Jap camp commandant at Kanyu openly admitted that the general in charge of the railway had said that he did not mind what happened to the prisoners – the railway must go through as fast as possible. Harry finally died, quite quickly, of dysentery and malaria. It is pathetic to read his constant thoughts of his family.

There have been no aeroplanes at all over for some days – an uncanny silence.

10 March 1945

The last of the parties for Ratburi has left. We have heard – in spite of Nobu-sawa's and Noguchi's assurances that the sick men who were compelled to go with these parties would not have to do any marching – that the first three parties had to do a march of 80 kilometres, while the later ones had to do perhaps 16–18 kilometres. When they arrived at their destination, there were no huts for them: but the majority were not put on to hut building – they were immediately taken to work on the aerodrome and had meanwhile to sleep in the open. They have no drugs there. Nobusawa told me himself that the parties need only take enough for the journey, and that as drugs would be supplied there they must not be taken from this camp. As one is always suspicious of assurances of this kind, we did give them various supplies to smuggle through but we could not risk giving them a great deal. Their rations are very poor – rice and salt, some beans occasionally, or dried veg. Under these conditions, with much malaria and little or no quinine, the phenomena of 1943 are occurring again – ulcers, exhaustion, anaemia, vitamin deficiencies.

The same state of affairs is reported from up-river camps, especially Rintin and Wampo – wretched rations and no medical supplies. Yet from the Dutch party at Ban Pong, where Velds is, comes news that the Nips' base depot there is full of quinine, plasmoquine and other drugs.

The wooden bridge has been repaired and is taking trains again.

Now that all the ditches round this camp have been finished and the Ratburi parties gone, things have become quieter and the demand for workers has eased off a little.

The Nips have cut down our monthly pay to 20 ticals instead of 30 – at a time when prices are going up. They say that they have discovered that officers at other camps have been paying high prices for *Bangkok Chronicles*, which they have forbidden in POW camps, and that it is therefore obvious that we are getting too much pay. Eggs are unobtainable at the moment – the Chinese dealer says the Jap army has commandeered all that are available, but this may be simply an excuse. We have no means of verifying it. We gather, however, that a considerable number of Jap troops are coming back into Thailand from Burma.

Some Red Cross stores which came into camp two weeks ago are still being held by the Japs. We need them badly, but they won't disgorge them.

12 March 1945

Nobusawa and Eda have started to go through the hospital patients, with a view to turning out as many as possible. They make all that can, walk 300–400 yards to the neighbourhood of Nobusawa's office, where as often as not they have to wait about for a long time before N and E condescend to appear. One doesn't send the very ill people, but there is a danger in keeping away too large a number, in case the Japs should suspect hanky-panky and take it out of the patients in consequence. It is an unedifying sight to see Nobusawa or Eda going rapidly through these queues of ill-looking, emaciated men, marking for discharge people whose condition in a civilised country would be marked for *urgent* admission to a hospital. Hinson and Bailey, two old patients of mine, are examples – marked for discharge yesterday by Eda, a mere NCO and a small farmer in civil life, in spite of all I could say. Actually these Nips make a point of *not* listening, and one often feels that by *not* speaking one may get better results.

We have had evidence recently that the Nip medical office alters our death certificates if they don't like the wording. 'Blackwater Fever' has been altered to 'Malaria' in several instances. It is not clear why they do this. Frequent incidence of blackwater fever, of course, tends to suggest inadequate treatment of malaria, but one doubts whether Nobusawa knows this. One can't feel that the alteration of these certificates really matters. We keep our own records (secret from the Nips, of course – a lot have already been safely buried where they can be recovered) and we have no reason to suppose that the data on death certificates which we give the Japs are communicated to the Red Cross or to our own authorities.

We have not yet had our February pay.

13 March 1945

The dog-faced 'general' was here today. Apparently on his round in the Jap part of the camp he found a party of Dutch sick from up-river dumped at the entrance of the camp: they had arrived about 4.30am and their Japanese guards had just left them there. Nothing had been done about getting them into the POW area of the camp. We did not even know they were there, as the Jap part of the camp is between our camp and the railway halt. He seems to have blown up the Jap administration over this and he actually apologised to Nor Punt, the Dutch interpreter.

Rations have been better in the last few days. It seems possible that some decision about closing down or reducing this camp has been reached by the 'general', as some pigs are being killed and the camp ducks are being distributed in rations.

An order has been issued that all knives and cutthroat razors have to be handed in to the Japanese. Furthermore, tomorrow all pens and ink are to be handed in, under threat of severe reprisals if any are found thereafter in the camp. So I think I shall bury this pen in a sealed bottle – I may be able to recover it later. I shall have to use pencil henceforward – until they are all called in too.

22 March 1945

All new sick in the camp now have to see Nobusawa before they can stop work. Each battalion medical officer takes his own along. The men are given marked wooden tallies according to whether they are to be hospital, bed-down in lines, one-hour or two-hour workers. Only in very exceptional circumstances will Nobusawa give a hospital or bed-down tally unless the battalion concerned, or the hospital, produces a 'recovered' man in exchange. The whole system of tallies has become so cumbrous and unwieldy that it lends itself to a good deal of jiggery-pokery, by which we contrive to avoid serious difficulties.[1]

[1] Note by RSH. Among other devices we had a number of extra (bogus) tallies but use of these had to be cautious as the Japs might check up on the total numbers at any moment if they became suspicious.

There were some bombers around about dawn this morning, but they seemed not to be after any fixed target – they did some shooting up of rolling stock with machine guns and cannon.

There is a rumour that a train up-country, which was carrying POWs, was shot up by a bomber with some casualties. Renes, one of the Dutch medical officers, is reported killed.

29 March 1945

A lot of aerial activity recently, but no attacks in this neighbourhood.

The Dutch party in Ban Pong reports that they have been handling consignments of American Red Cross packages. They say that the Nipponese have been pillaging these supplies – and consequently they have not felt it wrong to do so themselves.

Jock Sutherland has gone up-country with a party of 200, perhaps to Wampo.

1 April 1945

Aeroplanes about at breakfast time. One came directly overhead as I was frying an egg and a piece of rice bread, and dropped a cloud of leaflets. They were carried away from the camp by the wind, but a copy came into the camp later. There were some anti-Nip cartoons; the letterpress was in Burmese! – suitable for 1 April perhaps. We wonder whether the RAF think this is Burma? After lunch nine prisoners, wounded in an aerial attack up the line near Wampo, arrived down by diesel truck. One died shortly after arrival. A couple needed amputations. One was a Queensland aborigine, always a most cheerful and willing worker his comrades say. He will do all right.

These men were on a working party on the railway line near the Wampo viaduct, which they say was badly smashed up about a week ago; but the Nip in charge would not allow them to take cover, although there was plenty of time, for the plane circled round twice before attacking. They had to go on working – and one must admit the Nip himself stayed on. The bombs fell, killing some and injuring these others. The Nip was quite undamaged.

I received some letters and postcards from home today. I gather my second postcard got home in July '44.

Today all paper and pencils have to be handed in, under severe penalty.

3 April 1945

This morning between 9 and 11am a number of four-engined bombers (one painted black, the others grey-green) attacked Tamarkan bridge again. A good deal of damage was done to the wooden bridge, they say. Pamphlets were also dropped, giving a rough map of Burma, which shows our advance progressing – a cheering sight. We heard the sound of bombs up-river also.

6 April 1945

News has filtered down that a lot of damage was done to the viaduct at Wampo again.

Scenes in Chungkai camp, March 1945

Cemetery at Chungkai, 28 March 1945

Yesterday Ishikura ('Turtleneck', the disagreeable new Japanese official interpreter) divulged that a 'very fierce battle' was going on 'near Japan'. He also asked, it is said, what would be done with him if he were taken prisoner.

Half-day workers, in spite of Nobusawa's assurances to the contrary, are being marched the three miles to Tamarkan to work at repairing the bridge. To give Nobusawa his due, the decision to send them is not his, but that of the Japanese administrative side. The threat they use is that if they don't get enough 'half-day' workers for this purpose, they will take away all the cooks. This would cause hopeless disruption.

Nobusawa and Eda are evidently aware that the elaborate tally system gives us loopholes to protect our sick from being sent out to work, and are busily trying to devise a more effective machinery. We have the situation pretty well in hand, up to a point.

I have mentioned that from time to time the Nips have talked vaguely of giving us special foodstuffs for the sick, or some funds with which to buy eggs. They never actually give us anything, but their latest request – for detailed proposals as to what we want for the sick – makes one hope (moderately). I have drawn up an analysis of the present diet, and have made detailed proposals after consultations with the other medical officers, including the Dutch, for adequate ration scales. The number of items for which one might ask is limited by what we know of what is available. The chief items for which I have asked are kachang hijau (green lentils), peanuts, eggs, meat and fresh fruit. One is not at all confident that this will lead to anything, but one must make every attempt to get anything that there is a chance of getting.

11 April 1945

Word comes down from Captain Pitt's camp that treatment of the sick is as barbarous as ever – men are beaten up by the Jap medical sergeant simply for being sick. They are forced out to work and given tasks quite beyond their powers.

A few mangoes are ripening on the big tree in the cemetery near our hut – very delicious though small.

17 April 1945

Yesterday's theatre performance (simple songs and turns) was suddenly interrupted by Turtleneck, who strode up on to the stage in the middle of one of the early turns, slapped the surprised performers in the face and said that there must be no turns, only orchestral music. It was a surprise, because the script of the show had as usual been submitted to him for censoring and had been returned without comment. The show of course fizzled out. The performers say Ishikura was rather tight when he waded into them. Today orders have been issued that the theatre building is to be pulled down. The theory is, I think, that the Japs feel it is wrong for us to 'sing and be cheerful' when Japan is in difficulties. Sydney Nardell says that much the same occurred in his camp up-country, where the Jap commander complained that the men were singing 'as if they were winning', and all singing in camp, even religious services, was forbidden.

21 April 1945

Nobusawa is going through the hospital patients again, throwing out numbers of men who are far from well – such as Laird, who had blackwater fever badly some time ago, is still getting attacks of malaria and looks very thin and ill. But Nobusawa has put him down for two hours' work. These two-hour workers often in fact do a whole day's work, as the Nip administrative side are still demanding an exorbitant quota for full-day work, under pain of removing all our cooks. A lot of these full-day workers are made to do quite unnecessary digging and building jobs, just 'to keep them occupied'. Ishikura more or less admitted this the other day, saying to RSM Farmer, 'We' (Ishikura and Colonel Ishii, the group commander) 'do not agree with Colonel Yanagida's policy of treating you like gentlemen.' Ishikura told Edkins yesterday that Japan had broken off diplomatic relations with Russia as their behaviour was unsatisfactory. This is a surprising piece of news if true.

Today Nobusawa kept the 10 Battalion sick parade waiting for two hours in the square before he condescended to look at them.

27 April 1945

Two days ago at about 9pm Ishikura and Nobusawa sent for Colonel Hamilton (an Australian surgeon, senior medical officer in this camp) and notified him that he would be going next day to Non Pladuk with a working party of

200 as their medical officer – a job in fact for a junior medical officer. The day before, Colonel Hamilton had spoken to Lieutenant Otaki, a fairly reasonable Japanese officer on the administrative side, about the treatment of the sick up-country and about the two-hour workers being compelled by the Jap office to do full-day work. (Nobusawa knows perfectly well that the two-hour workers are being made to do a full day, but he continues to label men two-hour workers.) It is quite obvious that Ishikura and Nobusawa, annoyed by this perfectly justifiable complaint, have taken this petty and impertinent method of paying the colonel out. He asked why he, the hospital commandant, was being sent, and not one of the junior officers available. They replied that they thought he was the most suitable doctor to go – to look after a small party of 200.

A party of 200 sick down from Linson. They are all very anaemic, and many have well-marked beriberi. The Nips up there have green lentils but won't issue them.

3 May 1945

Two days ago Turtleneck told Edkins that he had heard 'as a rumour' that Germany had capitulated. This was confirmed by Mr Boon Pong, who came into the camp under close watch to deal with the canteen: he managed to let Clarkson see a slip of paper saying 'Germany has capitulated'. Turtleneck today says that a part of the German army under Hitler is continuing to resist, but the bulk of it has surrendered. Turtleneck says this will not make any difference to Japan, since Britain, Russia and America are certain to quarrel over Germany, and none will send troops to the East, for fear of hostilities in Germany. So they must at least have the idea that Japan is in some danger, though one feels they still think that at any moment Japan can call the whole thing off, 'shake hands', smile, stop fighting and retain all the territories which they have seized. They have surprises coming to them.

Colonel Hamilton has not actually left this camp yet, but Max Pemberton has taken over the command of the hospital group.

Nothing has happened as a result of the schedule of proposed hospital diets which I put forward some time ago. Ishikura refuses to discuss the question. My schedules have had to be altered to conform to Japanese scales of calorie values, which are obviously incorrect. For example, pork and coconut fat are shown on their scales as having a value of 0.7 calories per 1.0gm (instead of 9.0 calories) and they give green leaf vegetable (spinach, lettuce) the absurdly high value of 0.4 calories per 1.0gm.

17 May 1945

I am getting on with the digging of beds for growing kangkong (creeping spinach) to supplement the green lentil soup which is the main item of extra diet provided in the hospital from the secret fund which I administer. It seems not unlikely that we may get some 100-kilo sacks of green lentils from the Nips, purchased with 1,200 rupees of 'Burma' money which they took from the parties coming over to Siam after working on the Burma side of the railway. They called in all the Burma currency for changing to Siam currency when the parties came over, but refused to change this portion, because, they said, it must have been dishonestly come by, since the amount put in for changing was more than the whole groups had been paid in a month. One doubts this. They have now said that they are willing to use the money to buy us green lentils for the hospital. We have expressed warm approval of this plan. It seems very improbable that we shall ever get extra food for the sick out of Japanese-*owned* money. Another possible source of money which can be discussed as a means of helping the sick is the surplus in the working balance of the canteen. This, of course, has been built up solely out of POW money, out of the slight profits they make. We are using about 17 kilos of green lentils a day extra in the hospital at present, purchased out of the fund.

Ishikura said yesterday that the British and Americans had made a heavy attack on an island near Formosa and that the US fleet had had severe losses. A Nip sentry betrayed that the island was Okinawa. Nobusawa, asked by Ian in the lab the other day what was happening in the Philippines (we know of course that they are in MacArthur's hands) said that he had 'forgotten' the news from there.

Nobusawa and Eda came over the other day to tell Max that Colonel Ishii was going to give a prize of 30 ticals each week to the medical officer in charge of the battalion which had the fewest sick. Nobusawa thought this an excellent idea and suggested extending it to the hospital – a prize each week to the hospital medical officer who should discharge the most patients!

Colonel Hamilton has gone off with his party of 200 – to Tamuang apparently.

30 May 1945

All sorts of fantastic rumours, but in the absence of definite information from the Japanese we don't have any certain news. The up-river camps are very fertile sources of rumours – landings here, there and everywhere – which don't lose anything on their journey down here. Up-river camps on the railway are seeing large numbers of Japs, military and civil, some in very bad condition, coming down the railway out of Burma. They get little sympathy from the Japs in the camps through which they pass. People from the camp at Tarsao report that Subhas Bose was there for a few days on his way over to Thailand from Burma. One wonders where he will make for now.[1]

Desperately sick men continue to arrive here from up-country camps – the usual complaints, ulcers, vitamin deficiency, constant malaria, severe anaemia. New parties are formed from time to time to go up to replace these men sent down.

Nobusawa and Eda continue to pick out sick men for work. Yesterday they called on Max to produce a plan (a 'pran' as they pronounce it) for getting more men out to work. At the same time, Eda notified us that we must use less than 500gm of quinine a day though we actually need over 1,000gm.

There has been no progress with the provision of green lentils, or money to buy them with. The Jap administrative side now says that the money can't be changed! I suppose only a lunatic would buy Jap-sponsored Burmese currency now.

[1] The Indian nationalist leader left Bangkok on 18 June and was in Singapore at the time of the Japanese surrender. He tried to escape to Russia but the aircraft in which he was travelling crashed on its way to Formosa on 18 August 1945.

A fair quantity of Red Cross drugs have been handed over to us by the Japs. It is local stuff, collected by the Swiss Consul in Bangkok, but very useful – atebrin, iron, cod-liver oil and some miscellaneous special preparations collected from various Bangkok dispensaries.

6 June 1945

Four days ago Nobusawa issued an order that of the 600–700 sick men (and they were very sick) who came down recently from Aporon, Linson and Kwi, *at least 300* should now be marked fit for half-day work, as Colonel Ishii, he said, was going to HQ at Bangkok and must hand in better figures than were at present being shown. Nobusawa said that if we did not sort out 300, he would come himself and select more than that. What could we do? Nobusawa said that these half-day workers need only work for three days, and then he would let them back to bed. It has to be admitted that this group did actually only do half-day work for these three days, but yesterday, when Nobusawa was to have marked them sick again, he refused to see them at all, and today he refused to mark any of them sick.

Today, wonder of wonders, the Japs have actually handed over five 100-kilo bags of green lentils bought with the famous 'Burma rupees'. The money actually bought six, but the Japs are keeping one for themselves. This gives us 15 days' supply at 20 kilos a day – a most useful addition – and will enable me to conserve my dwindling 'secret' fund. The hospital has between 800 and 900 men in it, after Nobusawa's rigorous weeding out, and of these 400 will now get 50gm of green lentils a day. It makes a tremendous addition to their diet, supplying valuable protein and fat, and Vitamin B group. The cookhouse make it into a thick and very appetising soup, mixed with spinach (both the kangkong that I grow and wild spinach – *Amaranthus gangeticus* – which is collected by convalescent patients for small payments) and it is quite popular. Similarly, about 400 men in hospital get an egg a day, through the wangle which Clarkson runs in the canteen.

There has been a practically complete cessation of aerial activity for the last ten days – only an occasional recce plane seen.

The Koreans talk vaguely of an Allied landing in Borneo.

Tamuang

Tamuang

28 June 1945

The intervals between the entries in my notes have become longer than they used to be.[1] In the three weeks since my last entry, we have all left Chungkai camp and come down to Tamuang, recently vacated by 4 Group.

Tamuang camp, near the river bank between Kanburi and Ban Pong, covers an enormous area, surrounded and sub-divided by huge ditches. The hospital area alone is vast and it appears that 4 Group, once they got into this camp, had all the space, accommodation and camp labour that they required. They had only 18 deaths in all here in the last year. Their Japanese medical officer appears to have been knowledgeable and helpful, but was often obstructed by the Jap administrative side. Still, the hospital appears to have worked under pretty reasonable conditions.

I came down here by river barge the whole way, quite an interesting journey. The barge was crowded with hospital patients, who made the journey reasonably comfortably. The huts, when we got into them, were rather dilapidated but served. Now we are gradually settling down and getting things into order. We were able to bring over the unused portion of the five sacks of green lentils which we got from the Nips. There has been no progress with the proposal to use the canteen surplus for buying more.

Quinine has practically run out, except for a small secret 'last reserve' of a few kilos brought down here soldered in a tin disguised as coconut oil for cooking. We need at least 500gm a day but the Japs seem to have, or say they have, practically no supplies; on 24 June Eda gave us a bare kilo and said it must last us for five days, after which he might manage to obtain more. This morning he told Andy to go this afternoon to get quinine, as it had come. Andy went at 3.30, only to be told that today was a holiday – he must come tomorrow. Thus Nobusawa and Eda, sitting smoking in their office next door to the medical store.

Blitzing the hospital sick to provide workers continues here. Half-day workers are automatically upgraded to full-day workers after two days. Half-day workers, promised ten days' light work by Lieutenant Otaki, found themselves *next day* shifting heavy logs on the river bank.

On the 25th in the afternoon, bombers suddenly appeared in the skies, and the Tamarkan bridge area (now about 10 miles to the north of us) and the Kanburi area (slightly nearer, in the same direction) were heavily pounded.

---

[1] Note by RSH. The reason was the more frequent searches of the camp by the Koreans and Kempeitai. This made it necessary to keep papers and pencils better hidden, and it became inconvenient to get them out of hiding more often than necessary.

It is said that the wooden bridge was badly smashed, and the steel bridge still further damaged. A train was also shot up. Pamphlets were dropped, showing sea and air lines of attack developing towards Japan.

30 June 1945

Clarkson and Co. have got the canteen going again and we are able to obtain green lentils and eggs for the hospital. We have had fair supplies of powdered milk recently, made in China and sent in by the Swiss Red Cross people in Bangkok. It is invaluable for those who can't assimilate the normal diet. We have to be economical with it, however, as the quantity is limited and we don't want to run short. I control its issue, as I do that of the precious drugs and quinine. It takes a bit of time making fair allocations under changing conditions, but is the only way to avoid friction.

We medical officers are living in an extraordinarily small, uncomfortable and dirty hut. The hospital here holds about 720: there are a fair number of sick still to come from Chungkai, mostly people recently down from Aporon in Burma. The Japs have drastically curtailed our hospital area and accommodation by running a barbed wire fence across the area so as to cut off almost all the open space which was so pleasant when we came down first.

The officers in Kanburi, we hear, are shortly to begin to move to a new camp north or east of Bangkok.

11 August 1945

I have been busy with internal affairs in this camp, and I see it is well over a month since my last entry in this diary. There have been practically no signs of warlike activity in the neighbourhood. Some parties of sick have gone off in the last week or two to the big base hospital camp at Nakom Paton. Bob Brown, who has been pretty ill, probably amoebic hepatitis, went with the last party. Jock Sutherland died recently here, very unexpectedly.

Jack Masefield and Andy have left the camp to rejoin the officers. They kept on with us for a bit acting as dispensers in the hospital store: but finally, as they were not genuine medical officers, the Japs decided that they must go back to the officers' camp.

We have recently had an issue of a number of tins of American Red Cross food, about 12 tins between three people, and, still better, a fair number of Red Cross books – mostly American. One of them which I have read with special pleasure is *Heathen Days*, Mencken's latest volume of reminiscences – extremely amusing – in an American army edition. We have a new hut now, in which we have more room: and I've got a reasonably comfortable bed of flexible bamboo poles. I lost all the rope of which my previous bed was constructed on the journey down. But my bamboo and sacking chair arrived safely.

I have read a number of Dutch novels – and I converse with moderate fluency in Dutch now. De Fluiter has been very good about teaching me once or twice a week for the last six months or so.

There are rumours of all sorts – of terrific air raids on Japan, of peace feelers, of phenomenal advances. There are rumours of more Red Cross stuff for us at Bangkok. We have actually had 30 cases of American Red Cross drugs handed over to us by the Nips in the last few days. Vast quantities of disinfectant in tins; a lot of sterile normal saline for intravenous infusion – useful if we were having a cholera epidemic now; huge quantities of Vitamins A and D (not the ones we are short of!); and a lot of Multivits (very valuable) and Vitamin B for injection (invaluable). We think the Nips are holding about 50 more cases, some of which contain drugs desperately needed, but we have not been able to get them as yet. We know they are there, because our own people unloaded them in the Nips' store and had time to glance at some of the lists of contents. They may want to send some to other camps. But they ought to let us know what there is, so that we could decide how to divide them up. One can't rely on the Japanese to do that properly, as their choice of the packages they have issued to us shows.

The Nips have also, we know, quite large stores of American Red Cross clothing and boots but won't issue them, although a great number of men in this camp are desperately lacking in clothes.

The Japanese have at last agreed to our buying green lentils and eggs for the hospital from the canteen surplus – anything up to 8,000 ticals are available. This has been a great relief, though the Nips don't let us buy as much as we could wish. They allow us six 100-kilo bags of green lentils per month; and 200 eggs a day. This does a tremendous lot of good. We get extra eggs as well from the canteen by an arrangement not permitted by the Nips and my fund supplements the green lentils when necessary. At present nearly everybody in hospital benefits – we give 50gm of green lentils daily to about 600 men. A few days ago Nobusawa asked for 'suggestions' for spending 1,800 ticals per 14 days on extra food. I put in a schedule at once but nothing has come of it. There are still a lot of very sick men at up-river camps but for some time no party of sick has come down, to this camp at least.

Ishikura is said to have let it be known that Colonel Ishii thinks the war will be over by November – with what result he did not say. We live in hopes of an early release, but without any very great conviction. Another spell of cold weather with the clothing we have now will be unendurable. The Japanese have been putting quite a lot of camp working parties on what they call 'beautification' – one undertaking consists of building an elaborate curved bamboo bridge over a duckpond. Sometimes we feel they are trying to get the place to look a bit better in case the war ends, and then we decide that that is only wishful thinking.

17 August 1945

Yesterday, after several days in which rumours were quite subdued, there were great comings and goings. Ishii went off, they said to Bangkok, excitement grew, a small party was brought in from another camp, who said they had heard the Japanese were giving in . . . then a high Japanese officer arrived and was closeted with the Jap officers in their camp. Finally RSM Edkins was called across to the Japanese office, and briefly informed that the war was over and that we would now come under our own discipline.

Edkins came straight across to the hospital area, where a concert was in progress, and made the announcement to the audience. There was a tremendous burst of cheering. The National Anthems of Britain, Holland and the United States were sung, and then 'Abide with me'. One's emotions were almost numb, after such long suppression of hopes and fears. One could hardly realise that the moment for which one had waited with such desperate but such doubtful hopes had come at last. It was over: we were free again, and would soon be in touch with the outside world, home. It was almost impossible to grasp – at such a moment surely one should feel some overwhelming emotion: one just felt rather numb, rather shaky and rather inclined to sob. *Sunt lacrimae rerum, et mentem mortalia tangunt*[1] – that nebulous expression of half-comprehended emotion seemed exactly to express one's feeling, as one tried to grasp what had happened . . . and as one thought of friends who had earlier looked forward to the same release but had found a different one – John Daly, Harry Malet – and men who had died in hospital, in despair or snuffed out suddenly like Millar, the miner from Dalkeith, at Wan Tow Kien that night in February 1943.

25 August 1945

Discipline in the camp has been good since the Nipponese ceased to be our masters. Edkins has handled the situation extremely well, and one must admit that the Japanese have behaved with great restraint. They have kept right away from us so far as possible: but have maintained our food supplies.

Lea has been investigating the medical supplies held by the Japanese – Nobusawa's stores. They have handed over the balance of the Red Cross packing cases – any amount of atebrin, iron, vitamins, in fact everything we need. Why on earth could they not have let us have them at once? They also gave us three 5-kilo tins of quinine sulphate.

Three days ago the Bangkok Red Cross Commissioner (the Swiss Consul) came here to see us and walked round the hospital. The next day Nobusawa produced seventeen 5-kilo tins of quinine. The Jap administrative side the same day handed over 35,000 ticals of Red Cross money which they had been holding (we wonder for how long) without letting us know anything about it, or doing anything with it. They also issued large quantities of American Red Cross clothing, which has since been distributed.

1 September 1945

A British officer, dropped by parachute near a guerilla camp 20 kilometres away from here, has reached us – Ross, a very pleasant chap, who gets no peace with all the questions people are always asking him. We are able to get out of the camp into the village of Tamuang at times, and I have been once or twice to the Presbytery, in which live two Italian Roman Catholic priests, who have been here for many years.

We have been able to contact other camps in the vicinity – I have seen Perkins, McCutcheon and others at Kanburi.

Sick men from up-country are coming down as fast as they can be brought; and the shocking condition in which many of them are revives one's feelings of animosity against the Japanese, which had sunk quite low, seeing them so submissive and orderly and now harmless.

[1] 'Human deeds have their tears, and mortality touches the heart.' Virgil, *Aeneid* i.462

Top: Tamuang, 16 September 1945. Bottom: Kanburi, 15 September 1945

6 September 1945

Dakota transport planes, called up by Ross on his radio transmitter, have dropped good supplies of milk and food, drugs and clothes, blankets – everything we need. Representatives from the airborne troops that have been landed in Bangkok have come out to us here; a doctor, too, from the outside world. Men are now being taken in to Bangkok, by train mostly, to be flown out to Rangoon and the wide world again.

Appendix

Appendix

In the course of time the hospital camps worked out a system of deception of the Japanese by false enumeration of sick, so that when there was a blitz men who were more or less recovered but still classed as hospital cases (quite reasonably) could, at a pinch, be substituted for men marked by the Japanese as fit for work. The art was not to have more men in the 'recovery' category than was essential but still sufficient. This margin for substitution by the medical staff was often enough kept from our own administration in case they should inadvertently say or do anything which would bring down on them – or us – the wrath of the Japanese. Where I was responsible (as I was at Takanun most of the time) for giving the Japanese the camp's sick-malaria figures at intervals of 4–5 days in order to enable them to work out our ration of quinine tablets, I had to make sure that where checks were possible the figures tallied and that the malaria figures were plausible. These statements and figures and the connected arguments with the Japanese were complicated and exacting. I used to think that after these experiences I would never be able to tell the truth plainly again.

The calculation of the amount of quinine due for any given period depended on:

(a) The number of men working (who were supposed to get one quinine tablet – prophylactic – a day) and

(b) The number of men sick with malaria (who were supposed to get 15gm a day for 3 to 5 days). Neither quantity was of course effective and to endeavour to secure that the sick men should get 25–30gm a day for five days (and be off work for that time) it was necessary both to inflate the number of malaria cases and also to withhold 'prophylactic' quinine from a substantial proportion of the fit men. The difficulty and danger of this was that the Japanese medical office was liable to ask prisoners if they were getting their quinine daily. This entailed reliable cooperation from battalion officers and men who might be interrogated when in fact they were *not* getting quinine – for they had to understand that they *ought* to be getting it and also had to believe what was in fact true, that if they did not get it they were really no worse off. We had the belief that the blackwater fever which occurred so frequently and was so disastrous was often *due* to the fact that the sufferer had been taking inadequate prophylactic doses (which 3gm daily certainly was), in other words that the disease on top of the so-called prophylaxis was potentially more dangerous than the disease would be without it. The figures given over a period to the Nips enabled us to build up a certain reserve for emergencies, for sudden arrivals or for parties going away, for whom the Nips were indisposed to make special issues.

Biographical Index

Abron
59

Adachi
Imperial Japanese Army. English interpreter.
50, 96, 102, 144

Adams, G B ('Bill')
Asiatic Petroleum Company (Siam) Ltd, Bangkok.
Captain. Thai linguist.
51, 59, 65, 71, 78, 81, 83, 106, 138, 155

Adams, James
Dromedary farmer in Queensland. Lieutenant,
Federated Malay States Volunteer Force.
69, 81, 108

Anderson, Alexander ('Andy')
Glaxo representative in India. Second Lieutenant,
16th Punjab Regiment. Dispenser, No. 2 Group
Hospital, Chungkai, 1943–1945.
156, 159, 173, 174

Andrews
Captain, Federated Malay States Volunteer Force.
58, 59, 65

Angier, Gerald E
Planter, Bukit Mertajam Rubber Company Ltd,
Kedah. Captain, Pioneer Corps.
91

Archer, A L
Assistant Manager, Rubber Estates of Malaya Ltd,
Kota Tinggi, Johore. Staff Sergeant, Johore
Volunteer Engineers.
133

★Arkush, David
Captain, Army Dental Corps. Dental Officer,
Chungkai, August 1942–June 1945.
23, 59, 72

Aylwin, Claude Derek Lawrence
Captain, Royal Marines. Commanded Royal Marine
detachment in HMS *Prince of Wales* and, after her
sinking in December 1941, a rifle company made up
of survivors. This was merged with the remnants of
the 2nd Battalion, The Argyll and Sutherland
Highlanders, to form part of 'The Marine Argyll
Battalion', popularly known as 'The Plymouth
Argylls'.
22

Bailey
Royal Army Medical Corps.
162

Balfour, K
Manager, The Rubber Trust Ltd, Bukit Sembilan
Estates, Kedah. Kedah Volunteer Force.
51, 54

Barber
106, 108

Beautement, Cyril
Planter, Socfin Company Ltd, Kuala Lumpur. 2nd
(Selangor) Battalion, Federated Malay States
Volunteer Force.
137

Beeley, Frederick
Pathologist, Rubber Research Institute of Malaya,
Kuala Lumpur. Gunner, Light Artillery Battery,
Federated Malay States Volunteer Force. Died at
Kanyu, 30 June 1943.
109

Bellingham Smith, Oliver
Manager, Borneo Motors Ltd, Kuala Lumpur.
Captain, 2nd (Selangor) Battalion, Federated Malay
States Volunteer Force. Died at Kanyu, 11 June 1943.
107, 108, 112

Benson, Donald
Captain, Royal Army Medical Corps.
148, 155

★Black, Duncan McCallum
Major, Indian Medical Service. 12th Indian General
Hospital, 1939. Officer Commanding Ambulance
Train in Malaya, 1941. First medical officer to be sent
to Thailand. Senior Medical Officer, Ban Pong,
1942–1943.
23, 37, 46, 50, 52, 53, 54, 56, 57, 59, 61, 65, 69, 71,
72, 77, 78, 83, 94, 101, 103, 107, 137, 152, 159

Blomfield, Sidney Essex
Planter, Ladang Geddes, Dunlop Plantations Ltd,
Bahau, Negri Sembilan. Sergeant, 3rd (Negri
Sembilan) Battalion, Federated Malay States
Volunteer Force.
78

Boon Pong, *see* **Sirivejjabhandu**

Bose, Subhas Chandra
Formerly Mayor of Calcutta and President of the
All-India Congress. Leader of the 'Free India'
movement and organiser of the Indian National
Army.
169

Boswell
Quartermaster, No. 2 Group.
65

Braham, Mark Gordon
Captain, 1st Field Ambulance, Royal Army Medical Corps. Drowned when the *Hofuku Maru*, carrying 1,300 British prisoners of war on their way to Japan, was sunk by American bombers off Manila, 21 September 1944.
142

Britt, Leo E
Professional actor. Corporal, Royal Army Service Corps.
130, 140

Broughton, Thomas Richard
Major, Royal Scots.
65

★**Brown, Robert**
Captain, 6th Battalion, 1st Punjab Regiment. 'Officer orderly', Chungkai.
174

Calderwood, Robin W
Federated Malay States Police. Captain, 2nd Battalion, The Argyll and Sutherland Highlanders.
158

★**Cameron, Duncan**
Brother of Dr Ian Cameron. Manager, Estates Agency Department, Guthrie and Company Ltd, Kuala Lumpur. Returned to the United Kingdom for health reasons, May 1941.
125

Cameron, Ian Gordon
Senior partner in the medical practice in Kuala Lumpur which Robert Hardie joined in 1937. Retired, 1939, and returned to the United Kingdom.
125

★**Cameron, Margaret**
Wife of Duncan Cameron. Left Malaya with her husband, May 1941.
92, 125, 145

Cator, A C A ('Tony')
Captain, 2nd Battalion, The East Surrey Regiment.
143

★**Cayley, Ford Everard de Wend**
Captain, Royal Army Medical Corps. Medical Officer, 5th Battalion, The Suffolk Regiment. Awarded the MBE for his services as a prisoner of war.
48

Chapman, Dr Geoffrey Walter
Soils Officer, Serkam Division, Malacca Rubber Plantations Ltd, Malacca. Private, 4th (Malacca) Battalion, Straits Settlements Volunteer Force.
112

Chapman, John William
Captain, 2nd Battalion, 1st King George V's Own Gurkha Rifles. Sent with a party of British prisoners of war to Japan, 1944.
138

Chotani
Japanese sergeant.
45

Churchill, William Foster Norton ('Tony')
Commissioner of Lands and Mines, Trengganu. Interned in Changi civilian internment camp, 1942–1945. Distant relative of Winston Churchill.
16

Clark, Stanley James
Manager, Planters' Stores and Agency Company Ltd, Kuala Lumpur. Staff Sergeant, Federated Malay States Volunteer Force. Died at Chungkai, 31 August 1943.
78, 112

★**Clarke, Bertram John ('Blondie')**
Lieutenant, 4th Battalion, The Suffolk Regiment.
130, 146

Clarkson, J H
J A Russell and Company Ltd, Kuala Lumpur. Private, 2nd (Selangor) Battalion, Federated Malay States Volunteer Force.
137, 149, 155, 157, 159, 168, 170, 174

Cliffe, C Eric
Lieutenant, Royal Army Service Corps.
140

Cole, Walter
Assistant Adviser, Kemaman, Trengganu. Lieutenant, 2nd Battalion, The Argyll and Sutherland Highlanders. Died at Takanun, 31 May 1943.
95

Cooper, The Rt. Hon Alfred Duff DSO MP
Chancellor of the Duchy of Lancaster, 1941–1943. Resident Minister of State, Singapore, August 1941–January 1942.
15

Cooper, Lady Diana
Wife of Alfred Duff Cooper.
15

Corke, Clive G
Planter, Teluk Datoh Estate, Banting, Selangor. Major, 2nd (Selangor) Battalion, Federated Malay States Volunteer Force.
78, 81

Cornelius, William Hern
Lieutenant-Colonel, Royal Army Medical Corps. Assistant Director of Medical Services, HQ Medical Base Singapore District, December 1941–February 1942.
18

Cowell, Frederick
Private, 2nd Battalion, The Loyal Regiment (North Lancashire). Died at Kanburi, 12 October 1942.
48

Cruickshank, Eric Kennedy
Captain, Royal Army Medical Corps. Medical Specialist, Changi camp, 1942–1945.
19

★**Cumming, Robert Alexander**
Squadron Leader, Medical Branch, Royal Air Force. Pathologist, No. 1 Allied General Hospital, Java. Awarded the OBE for his services as a prisoner of war.
158

Currie, A M R ('Sandy')
Standard Bank of India, Australia and China, Singapore. Lieutenant, Machine Gun Company, 1st Battalion, Straits Settlements Volunteer Force.
51

Daly, Augustine Joseph ('John') MC
Stockbroker, Charles Bradbourne and Company Ltd, Kuala Lumpur. Captain, 3rd Malayan Field Ambulance, Federated Malay States Volunteer Force. Died at Chungkai, 15 May 1944.
15, 19, 22, 23, 137, 140, 176

Davies, Geoffrey Manning
Captain, Royal Army Medical Corps.
23, 51, 54

de Fluiter, H J
Royal Netherlands East Indies Army. Entomologist.
144, 157, 174

de Marco, Dom
Chartered accountant, Whittall and Company, Kuala Lumpur. Private, Machine Gun Company, 3rd (Selangor) Battalion, Federated Malay States Volunteer Force.
78

*de Wardener, Hugh Edward ('Ginger')
Captain, 198th Field Ambulance, Royal Army Medical Corps. Awarded the MBE for his devotion to duty in the treatment of cholera patients.
45, 95, 130, 133, 144, 159

*Desch, Gwen
Wife of Harold Desch. Left Malaya, April 1941, with her young son, travelling first to India and then, in the spring of 1942, to South Africa. Returned to the United Kingdom, October 1944.
131

Desch, Harold Ernest
Forest Research Officer (Wood Technologist), Colonial Forest Service, Malaya, from 1932. Federated Malay States Volunteer Force. Prisoner of war, Changi, 1942–1945.
16, 21, 22

Donaldson, William
Captain, Royal Army Medical Corps. Physician, Nakom Paton base hospital.
133

*Douglas, Thomas Pittendrigh
Lieutenant, Royal Corps of Signals, Malaya Command Signals. BBC engineer before the war. Built and operated a secret radio receiver on the railway, now in the Royal Corps of Signals Museum, Blandford. Awarded the MBE for his services as a prisoner of war.
109

du Boulay, Henrietta
Wife of Noel du Boulay of Torkington Estate, Sabak Bernan, Selangor.
16

Dunlop, Alexander Louden
Malayan Medical Service. Estate Medical Officer, United Patani Rubber Estates, Sungei Patani, Kedah. Major, Royal Army Medical Corps. Senior Medical Officer, III Indian Corps, Changi. Hospital Registrar, Chungkai, 1945.
152, 153

Dunlop, Ernest Edward
Lieutenant-Colonel, Australian Army Medical Corps. OC, 2/2nd Casualty Clearing Station, 8th Australian Division, 1941–1942. Senior Medical Officer, Chungkai, January–May 1944. Awarded the OBE for his services as a prisoner of war.
137

Eda, Asaichi
Sergeant-Major, Imperial Japanese Army. Sentenced to death for ill-treatment of prisoners of war, June 1946.
52, 53, 105, 107, 116, 131, 143, 146, 156, 159, 162, 166, 168, 173

Edgar, A T ('Sandy')
Manager, Dindings Rubber Estates Ltd, Suffolk Estate, Sitiawan, Perak. Author of *Rubber Planting in Malaysia*. Major, 2nd (Selangor) Battalion, Federated Malay States Volunteer Force.
78

Edkins, Ernest William
Sergeant, 2nd Battalion, The North Staffordshire Regiment. Company Sergeant-Major Instructor, Straits Settlements Volunteer Force, 1939. Regimental Sergeant-Major in charge of Chungkai and Tamuang camps, 1945.
161, 167, 175, 176

Elvidge, John William
Driver, Royal Corps of Signals, Malaya Command Signals. Died at Ban Pong, 8 December 1942.
55

Emery, Edward Joseph
Medical partner of Robert Hardie in Kuala Lumpur. Captain, Royal Army Medical Corps.
133

Epstein, William Abraham
Captain, Medical Corps, United States Navy. Commanded the Naval Dispensary at Manila, Philippine Islands, 1940. Senior Medical Officer, USS *Houston*. Survived the sinking of the *Houston* on 28 February 1942 but later captured by the Japanese and taken to Java. Prisoner of war in Singapore and, from January 1943, on the Burma-Siam railway.
159

Evans, Donald Kingsford
Asiatic Petroleum Company Ltd, Singapore. Lieutenant, Singapore Royal Artillery, Straits Settlements Volunteer Force. Died at Takanun, 31 May 1943.
95

*Farmer, Samuel Edward
Regimental Sergeant-Major, Royal Corps of Signals, Malaya Command Signals.
167

Finegold, Martin Emanuel
Second Lieutenant, Royal Indian Army Service Corps.
138

Robertson, Alan G
Chartered accountant, Neill and Bell, Kuala Lumpur. Sergeant-Major, 3rd Malayan Field Ambulance, Federated Malay States Volunteer Force.
131

Robertson D G
Manager, Sembilan Estate, Kuantan Rubber Company Ltd, Kuantan, Pahang. Brother of Alan Robertson.
78

★Robey, Mervyn Errol Leveson ('George')
Superintendent, Ledang Geddes, Dunlop Plantations Ltd, Bahau, Negri Sembilan. Lieutenant, 2nd Battalion, The Malay Regiment.
107

Robson, Cedric Rowntree
Captain, 5th Casualty Clearing Station, Royal Army Medical Corps. Drowned when the *Hofuku Maru*, carrying 1,300 British prisoners of war on their way to Japan, was sunk by American bombers off Manila, 21 September 1944.
61, 142

Rogers, M F
Planter, Voules Estate, Kepong (Malay) Rubber Estates Ltd, Tenang, Johore. Private, 2nd (Selangor) Battalion, Federated Malay States Volunteer Force.
85

Romney, Percy Hall
Assistant Editor, *The Malay Mail*, Kuala Lumpur. Company Sergeant-Major, Machine Gun Company, 2nd (Selangor) Battalion, Federated Malay States Volunteer Force.
78

Ross
Lieutenant.
176, 178

Ross, H T ('Tommy')
Federated Malay States Government Press, Kuala Lumpur. 2nd (Selangor) Battalion, Federated Malay States Volunteer Force.
65, 66

Russell, John W
Chartered accountant, Dunlop Plantations Ltd, Malacca. 4th (Malacca) Battalion, Straits Settlements Volunteer Force.
51, 108

Rutty, Jack
Australian. Planter, Pahang. Sergeant, 4th (Pahang) Battalion, Federated Malay States Volunteer Force.
51

Saito
Lieutenant, Imperial Japanese Army. Medical Officer.
52

Sakai
Captain, Imperial Japanese Army.
56

Sandeman, Hugh A
Planter, Negri Sembilan. Lieutenant, 2nd Battalion, The Malay Regiment.
130

Seed, Charles W S
Acting Deputy Auditor, Colonial Audit Department, Kuala Lumpur.
16

Shannon, Hugh Goddard
Manager, North Malay Rubber Estates Ltd, Kedah. Lieutenant, Royal Army Ordnance Corps. Died on the railway, 4 April 1944.
51

Shearlaw, Peter W
Planter, Vallambrosa Rubber Company Ltd, Selangor. 2nd (Selangor) Battalion, Federated Malay States Volunteer Force. Liaison officer with the British Battalion.
65, 140

Shearman, Percy Herbert
Sergeant, 5th Battalion, The Suffolk Regiment. Hospital orderly on the railway. Awarded the BEM for his services as a prisoner of war.
78, 81, 86, 100

Sinclair, K G
Assistant General Manager, Planters' Stores and Agency Company Ltd, Kuala Lumpur. Lance-Corporal, 2nd (Selangor) Battalion, Federated Malay States Volunteer Force.
78

Sirivejjabhandu, Boon Pong
Thai merchant from Kanchanburi, underground agent and captain in the Free Siamese Army. Supplied the camps at the southern end of the railway with such rations as the Japanese permitted; also at great personal risk cashed cheques, brought in secret medical supplies and advanced money against personal valuables, which he scrupulously redeemed after the war. Awarded the George Medal for his services and courage.
81, 168

Skinner, Cyril Gordon
Captain, 2nd Battalion, The Argyll and Sutherland Highlanders. Liaison officer and interpreter at No. 2 Group Headquarters, July 1942 to February 1945. Awarded the MBE for his services as a prisoner of war.
50, 53, 92

Smith, Norman
Second Lieutenant, 5th Searchlight Regiment, Royal Artillery.
140

★Smith Laing, Brownlow North ('Brownie')
Manager of a Guthrie estate, Negri Sembilan. Lieutenant, 3rd (Negri Sembilan) Battalion, Federated Malay States Volunteer Force. Liaison officer with the 2nd Battalion, The Cambridgeshire Regiment.
48, 51, 58, 61, 66

Spong, Robert Albert
Private, 4th Ordnance Stores Company, Royal Army Ordnance Corps. Drowned when the *Hofuku Maru*, carrying 1,300 British prisoners of war on their way to Japan, was sunk by American bombers off Manila, 21 September 1944.
138

Webber, Max L
Forestry Service, Federated Malay States. Captain, 2nd Battalion, The Loyal Regiment (North Lancashire). With his brother Donald, he operated one of the most successful secret radio sets in No. 2 Group on the railway, distributing over 700 news bulletins to Chungkai and other camps. Awarded the OBE for his courage and devotion to duty.
137

Weir
Orderly, Royal Army Medical Corps.
42

Wells, Charles
Malayan Veterinary Service. Captain, 3rd (Negri Sembilan) Battalion, Federated Malay States Volunteer Force.
105

Welsh, Robert Beall Colville
Captain, Royal Army Medical Corps.
55

★West, George Francis ('Paddy')
Estate Medical Practitioner, Bukit Rotan, Kuala Selangor. Medical Officer, Socfin Company Ltd. Lieutenant-Colonel, 3rd Malayan Field Ambulance, Federated Malay States Volunteer Force. Prisoner of war, Sumatra, 1942–1945. Awarded the OBE for his services.
16

White, J Glyn
Lieutenant-Colonel, Australian Army Medical Corps. Deputy Assistant Director Medical Services, 8th Australian Division, 1941.
20

Wild, Cyril Hew Dalrymple
Major, 4th Battalion, The Oxfordshire and Buckinghamshire Light Infantry. Staff officer with III Indian Corps during the Malayan campaign. Japanese linguist: acted as interpreter at the Singapore surrender. Interpreter again at the Japanese surrender in 1945, when he produced the Union Jack which he had carried on 15 February 1942. Awarded the MBE for his war services. War Crimes Liaison Officer (with the rank of colonel), Allied Land Forces, South East Asia. Killed in an air crash at Hong Kong, 26 September 1946.
121

Williams, Bill
Soils chemist, Rubber Research Institute, Kuala Lumpur.
144

Williamson, John Rowley
Lieutenant-Colonel, Royal Indian Artillery. British camp commandant, No. 2 Group, June 1942–February 1945, in command of some 14,000 officers and men. Awarded the DSO for services in Malaya.
35, 50, 52, 53, 54, 58, 59, 92, 131, 149, 150, 151

Woods, Everard
Major, Royal Army Service Corps. Learnt to play chess while a prisoner on the railway and after the war competed in the Hastings International Chess Congress.
130

Woodward, Frank J
Solicitor, Bannon and Bailey, Kuala Lumpur. Armoured Car Company, Federated Malay States Volunteer Force.
137, 149, 157, 159

Wright, Nigel
Botanist, Rubber Research Institute, Kuala Lumpur.
112, 138, 140

Yanagida, Shoichi
Lieutenant-Colonel, Imperial Japanese Army. Commander of No. 2 Group. Sentenced to 20 years' imprisonment for ill-treatment of prisoners of war but subsequently pardoned.
57, 86, 95, 102, 144, 147, 150, 167

Editor's Note

Decorations (where known) and ranks are contemporary with this account. In addition to those whose names are marked with an asterisk, I am particularly indebted to the following for their help: Telfer Dunbar, Ewart Escritt, Sir William Goode, Gwendolen Grieve, Charles Kinahan, Cecil Lee, Eric Lomax, Jim Rea, Dr Alfie Roy, John Sharp, Jim Tough and Douglas Weir. CD

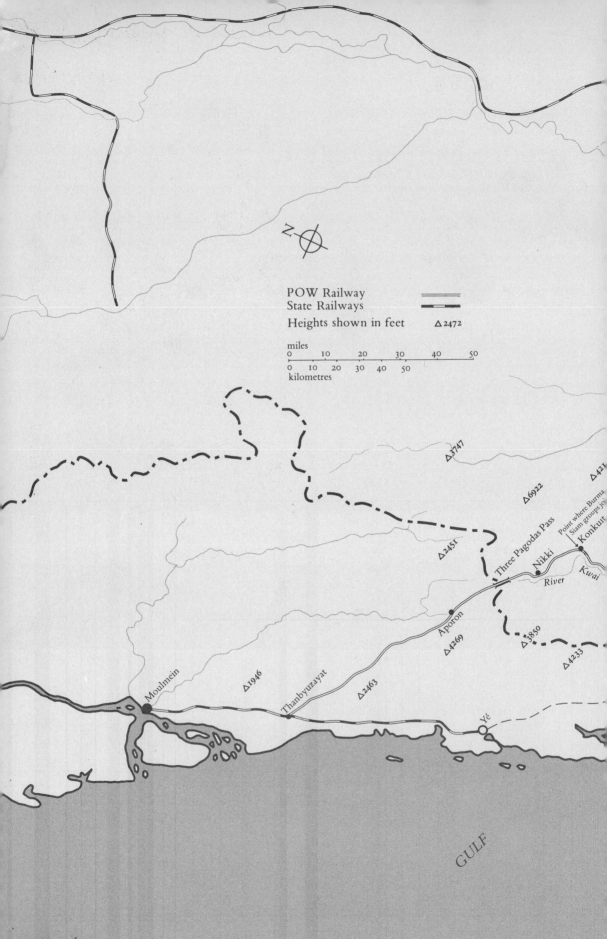

POW Railway
State Railways
Heights shown in feet △ 2472

miles
0   10   20   30   40   50
0   10   20   30   40   50
kilometres

△ 3747

△ 6922   △ 421

△ 2451   Point where Burma
                Siam groups jo
          Three Pagodas Pass   Konkuit
                    Nikki
                  River   Kwai

          Aporon
          △ 4269   △ 3850
                             △ 4233
Moulmein   △ 1946
          Thanbyuzayat   △ 2463
                              Yé

GULF